I See You

HELPING MOMS GO
FROM OVERWHELMED TO
IN CONTROL

by
meagan ruffing

i

I See You
© 2016 Meagan Ruffing

Print ISBN: 978-1- 937660-98- 7
eBook ISBN: 978-1- 937660-994

Published by:
Heritage Press Publications, LLC
PO Box 561
Collinsville, MS 39325

Some names and identifying details have been changed to protect the privacy of individuals.

Credit: *PCIT Treatment Manual: Session Outlines*, pg. 21-25, Sheila M. Eyberg, 1999.

Revelation 12:11 says that "they overcame by the blood of the lamb and the word of their testimony." I've always been intrigued by the pronouns "they" and "their" in this verse as they allude to the notion that we're fighting, and thus winning, together. To me, *I See You* by Meagan Ruffing is her sharing her testimony in a way that is not only freeing and empowering for her, but also for her readers. She begins part one by sharing that this book is intended to tell parents that it's going to be okay, that there's hope, and that they're not failing. Meagan goes on to share a very candid, raw view into raising her son Dylan. I absolutely loved how Meagan intertwined tips, definitions, resources, and encouragement throughout her story. While I enjoy purely educational books as a resource, I often just want to read a story. Meagan cleverly taught along the way while telling a true and compelling story. I couldn't put her book down! As a children's ministry director, I felt empowered with fresh ideas and perspective after reading this book.

Fellow overcomers, you won't want to miss *I See You.*

Margo White
Catalyst Children's Pastor

Meagan Ruffing offers a rare and honest glimpse into the daily routine of raising a special needs child. Her encouragement is a gift to parents, whether they know what's going on with their child or are struggling to find answers as she was. In addition to being an invaluable resource for parents of special needs children, *I See You* should be required reading for the rest of us. *I See You* has made me a more grateful mother and a more understanding member of the community of parents. On top of all that, it's just a great narrative. Ruffing's story kept me turning pages, cheering for her and her family to find their answers. The resources complete the gift Ruffing has provided us. I predict she will help many who are facing similar situations.

> *Lela Davidson author of*
> **Faking Balance: Adventures**
> **in Work and Life**

In her poignant new book, *I See You*, author Meagan Ruffing pulls back the heavy curtain of secrecy and shame to show us a gritty side of parenting that many of us know little about (but should), and that many others will find all too familiar.

With refreshing transparency and a draws-you-in writing style, Ruffing explores what it means to raise a son with significant and complex behavioral challenges. While *I See You* tells the sometimes excruciatingly painful story of Dylan's struggles, it also reveals the often raw and ragged, but absolutely tender and unrelenting love of a mother who will not give up on this boy she gave life to—will not.

Meagan not only candidly chronicles what it's like to navigate the confusing maze of educational and medical options, she offers practical help and hope, along with invaluable resources, for those parents and families facing a similar situation with their beloved child.

praise for i see you

Reading *I See You* made me weep, squirm, and even laugh at times. And it made me think…how can I be a better support for the parents I know whose emotional and spiritual reserves are almost depleted from fighting for (and sometimes with) a child with behavioral challenges? But perhaps most surprisingly, it also made me thankful…thankful for a little boy like Dylan who bravely makes his way through day after difficult day, thankful for a mom like Meagan who loves without flinching through a kind of agonizingly painful parenthood she never could've imagined, and thankful for a faithful God who comes to us with a promise of renewed strength and breathtaking beauty, even in the extremes of brokenness.

Dr. Jodi Detrick ~ Writer, Speaker, Coach
Author of The Jesus-Hearted Woman

table of contents

foreword

Raising children is not for wimps.

It is hard, challenging, stretching you past the point you imagined you could be stretched.

It transforms you.

And that's just being the parent of what most people would call "typical" children.

So, what's it like when your child is not typical? When he or she is not developing as expected? What's it like when your child's behavior can't be laughed off as "boys will be boys?" What's it like for parents who have struggled with and studied all of the most popular parenting and discipline strategies...but then go to apply them and find they just don't work?

I See You is a heartfelt and ongoing journey of a determined mother's daily struggle to see past the smokescreens of behavioral outbursts, opposition, and sensory sensitivity in order to see her son, Dylan, more clearly. Her raw and honest descriptions allow readers a glimpse into the lived experience of those battling mental illness in their children, and in her search for light and hope in the midst of messy, raw life, she is able to give advice to parents struggling through a similar journey of their own.

Meagan's journey of attempting to partner with a broken healthcare system got my attention. Systems are not always user-friendly and are not developed enough to always meet families where they are living in the battle with behavioral and emotional challenges. She inspires me to advocate for better healthcare, for better systems, for more coordinated care, and for earlier detection and better evidence-based treatment for children and families suffering and fighting for a better tomorrow.

She courageously and honestly reflects on her experience in order to educate professionals and remind other parents that they are not alone. May Meagan's experience inspire you to keep fighting to celebrate your child, regardless of his or her skill level or challenge. May her work bring insight to professionals by recognizing the lived experience of so many of the families we treat. May we strive to do better and develop even more helpful information and treatments so that one day we can provide true partnership in full healthcare—addressing both medical and mental health.

Amy Vaughan, OTR/L, BCP
Occupational Therapist

special thanks and acknowledgments

There were so many different people along the way who encouraged me, helped me, spoke words of affirmation over me, and loved me while I wrote this book. Thank you to Theresa Jones for your friendship and unconditional love. I cannot imagine going through this mothering journey without you on the other end of the line. Thank you to my parents, Dawn Longley, Gary Longley, Anne Longley, and Rody Fuller. Thank you, Dad, for letting me cry on the phone to you when those tough parenting moments snuck up on me. Thank you, Anne, for offering words of encouragement. And thank you, Mom, for always being my number one fan. Thank you to my brother, Donny Longley, for helping me navigate the ADHD world with my son. You are a soft place to land when things get tough. Thank you to my sister, Laura Longley, who inspires me to be the best version of myself while loving me just as I am. And thank you for believing in me when I filled out that very first college application to my dream school from which I proudly earned a degree in journalism.

Thank you to my girls at Monett MOPS for being my first friends in Missouri. Thank you for walking with me in faith when I took my first steps to knowing Jesus. Katie Brittenham, Jessica Scott, and Phyllis Garrett: you will forever hold a special place in my heart. Many thanks to Jodi Detrick, Lela Davidson, Margo White, Gloria Dillen, Sara Snyder, Colleen Kern, April Fletcher, Lesli Lovler, Martha Rosse, Amy Vaughan, Michelle Deleva, Melinda Bunyard, Sue LeBreton, Laurie Fisher-Zottman, Sandi Haustein, Laura Reagan, Lisa Schlictman, Sherry Lotufo, and Tracy Novreske.

special thanks and acknowledgments

Thank you to Randy and Terrie Sexton for watching Hannah every week while we took Dylan to PCIT. But most of all, thank you for your friendship and wisdom. Thank you to Shannon Alexander, Jolene Palmquist, and Ron and Donna McNaughton for your friendship and for loving us just as we are.

To my writing coach, Christina Katz: thank you for gifting me with the Writer Mama Scholarship so that I could take my very first writing class with you. Your expertise in building platforms and teaching others how to write for RPPs has taught me so much.

Thank you to my editors, Nikki Hill and Hanne Moon, for believing in me enough to help me turn my words into a book. Thank you to my graphic designer, Veronica Zucca, for agreeing to jump on board with me while we navigated publishing a book together for the first time. Let's do it again!

Thank you to my Gram. You bring peace, contentment, and a feeling of home to me whenever I think of you. And thank you for being the very first person to ask for my autograph! Gabe, thank you for loving me just as I am. Thank you for always saying yes when I asked if I could run out for an hour or two to network with someone in my field. Thank you for always being my very first proofreader for everything I write, for encouraging me when I played the comparison game and for never questioning my dream to write this book.

special thanks and acknowledgments

To my kids, Dylan, Hannah, and Elinor, you are the answer to so many prayers. I love you. I am humbled by how many hands have guided me along the way and am forever grateful to each and every one of you for investing your time in me. Thank you.

Sincerely,
Meagan

introduction

Looking back, I realize how much I chose my time wisely when it came to reading books, and it wasn't always by choice. You see, I had to be picky. I had to have a book that I could pick up and put down at a moment's notice, because I didn't have much free time between fielding tantrums and staying sane. I never found the book I was looking for when my family and I were going through this journey with our son. We're still going through it, and the more I talk to other parents about their own trials with getting their children's diagnoses, the more I see a need for a balanced book that gives the reader personal testimony of the daily, in-the-trenches struggles we all go through, as well as provide simple ways for parents to pour back into themselves. After all, we can only give so much time, effort, and talent to our kids, and sometimes it's easy to forget that we must continually invest in ourselves if we ever want to see this through.

I have broken this book up into two parts. Part one will be my story about having my first child and noticing things in his behavior that I didn't understand. I go into detail about all of our doctors' appointments and the toll that took on our family—specifically, my marriage.

The second half of the book is all about going from overwhelmed to in control. Having a child who requires more attention than others can be a very stressful thing. Over the years, I have found ways to "lighten the load," so to speak, and give myself a much-needed break from the self-imposed feelings of thinking I am not a good enough mom to Dylan. Because in my many conversations with other moms, I found a common theme: we're all struggling in some way. Your child might not have special needs, but you might be going through something in your life that requires a bit more attention too. Because of that, maybe you feel yourself spinning out of control. I share my tips and tricks in this section of the book on how to handle that. After all, we can only pour out onto others what we've poured into ourselves.

My hope is that you find something within these pages that will help you, even if it is just one little nugget of hope when you feel like you just can't do it anymore, to help you get through parenting for another day. But perhaps, if we all stick together and share our stories, the burden just might become a little lighter for us all.

PART ONE

I'm writing the book that I have desperately been looking for. The one that tells parents that it's going to be okay and that there is hope.

The one that tells them that they aren't failing and that they are good parents, because, at the end of each day, it can feel very lonely.

I still see glimpses of my little boy. There are still times when the sweet side of him comes out and I think, There he is. *Those moments are just enough to help me make it through another day. This book has been many years in the making. However, the time has come for me to put fingers to keyboard and tell you my story and my son's story.*

This is the story of raising Dylan.

Naïve Bliss

"Being a mom has made me so tired. And so happy."

– Tina Fey

Dylan punched me today.

He punched me in the stomach because I tried to intervene when he and his friend were fighting over who should shut the door. Dylan has hit me almost every day for the past week, but today was a first, because today's hit was actually a punch, and it hurt.

Like, for real.

And he felt no remorse afterwards. I went upstairs to talk to him, but I couldn't control myself. I couldn't stop crying as the reality of what our lives have come to stared me straight in the face: me, the adult, afraid that my six-year-old son was going to hurt me, someone in our family, or one of his friends. It's possible. Just yesterday, I got a knock at the door from the neighbor girl telling me that Dylan was outside holding a box cutter, saying he wanted to get revenge on the boys in the neighborhood.

A punch doesn't seem nearly as bad as a box cutter, but today was my breaking point. I had to call in support, and Gabe came home after not being able to understand what I was saying on the phone. I know he's worried too. Thank God he came home and I was able to take a few moments to myself.

If you are a parent reading this book, you've probably already hit rock bottom or are close to it yourself. You're probably wondering—like I wondered—how you're going to help your child function so you can all have a normal life?

Normal.

Now there's a word with some weight behind it, and a word that probably grates like nails on a chalkboard at times. Everyone dreams of having a "normal" child, but what do you do when that just doesn't happen?

As you probably know by now, almost every question on the forms you have to fill out at therapists' offices and doctors' offices will ask you about your pregnancy. Was it normal? How long? Any odd cravings? Vaginal or caesarian? I used to think answering those questions would hold the answer to what was causing Dylan to act the way he does. Like a doctor would read them and say, "Oh, I see you had Dylan at thirty-eight weeks gestational. I know why he's behaving badly. It's because you were on Zoloft while you were pregnant. It's because you fell that one day at work while wearing your Dansko clogs." But my answers never held the key: vaginal birth, epidural, mom and baby doing great.

The day Dylan was born was one of the best days of my life—December 16, 2008, to be exact. Gabe and I had been trying for nearly two years to conceive a child. As stunned and excited as we were when that pregnancy test came back positive, it was nothing compared to how we felt when I went into labor. I remember it well, because my water broke while Gabe and I were sleeping on an air mattress in the spare bedroom. We were in the process of laying hardwood floors and the air mattress was where we were camping out while things were getting put back together.

A tiny pregnancy bladder was nothing new to me, but when I woke up in the middle of the night to go the bathroom, I couldn't seem to, well, stop going, if you know what I mean. So I woke Gabe up and told him I thought my water had broken.

"Oh, my gosh, oh, my gosh, oh, my gosh. Okay. Oh, my gosh. We're having a baby," he frantically whispered as he rushed to get ready.

I remember putting a towel down on the passenger's seat in the car so I wouldn't get the leather wet. I was scared, excited, and so ready to meet my son. Gabe and I call this time (actually the whole pregnancy and life before kids), naïve bliss. You think you know what it's going to be like. You dream about what it's going to be like and gush over making a child that will look like the both of you. It's something that has been created from the love of two people. You know it's possible, of course, but you never really think that anything will be wrong with your bouncing bundle of joy. But when you actually have the baby and you bring him home, and he won't stop crying and he won't sleep…like ever…you start to realize parenting is nothing like what you expected.

Those first few days and weeks were such a blur. Like most new parents, we were just trying to survive. We expected the lack of sleep, nightly feedings, and baby cuddles, but we didn't expect to have a baby who could not be soothed, didn't want to be held, and never seemed happy. It's hard for me to look back at pictures of Dylan when he was a few weeks old because he looks so unhappy. Before, I didn't think it was possible for a baby to look unhappy. I know now it is.

I started surfing the Internet on my phone when I nursed him to see if I could find something that might help me understand why he was crying all the time. I read about colic and sifted through the questions: has your baby been dropped, does he have an upset stomach, did you eat something that got through the breast milk that he might be allergic to, and on and on and on. I continually told his pediatrician that something just didn't seem right. I didn't think having a baby was supposed to be like this. It wasn't until my mother said something to me that I really knew something was off.

My mom was visiting, and she urged us to take some time alone together. Gabe and I went out to dinner for our first hour or two away since having Dylan. "I'll watch Dylan. He'll be fine," she said.

When we got home, I opened the door and heard the vacuum. Gabe and I knew without a doubt that he must have been screaming. The noise of the vacuum is supposed to sooth colicky babies, they say.

Yeah, right.

My poor mother was so distraught. "Something's not right, Meg. Babies don't cry this much. You need to take him to the doctor." I knew she was right, but what I didn't know then was that realization would change the rest of our lives.

8

Is it Colic? GERD? Or Both?

"A mother is one to whom you hurry when you are troubled."
– Emily Dickinson

One of the things I loved about Dylan's pediatrician was that she was thorough (even overly cautious at times), but in our case, that was good. When we told her about Dylan's crying, she recommended an upper GI study (upper gastrointestinal endoscopy) that would tell us if there was something going on in his intestines that would be making him so fussy. At six months old and never having had a bottle, I had to somehow get Dylan to drink a white, frothy beverage so the technicians could see where it traveled through his body. I did it, and we found out it was GERD (gastroesophageal reflux disease).

Basically, Dylan had silent reflux. Instead of spitting up after a feeding, the milk would come back up, but just enough to burn his throat before going back down into his stomach. Okay, wow! No wonder he was so upset. He had been uncomfortable since birth and the poor thing could not tell us that he was in so much pain. After putting him on Prilosec, things got better.

If you're reading this and your baby seems fussy—like, abnormally fussy—get him checked out for reflux. I can't tell you how many mom conversations I've sat in on, hearing the same story over and over again. I'd chime in and tell them, "It's probably reflux." Another tip: if you're nursing, stay away from acidic foods. What you eat, they eat too, so avoid foods that could aggravate any underlying condition. Also, when your baby is sleeping, put a wedge pillow underneath the crib mattress. This can lift the head just enough so that the acidity from the stomach won't be able to rise into the throat as much.

Babies with reflux also like to eat a lot, but not a lot at a time. They cluster feed, which means they eat a little at a time more often than other babies, which is why you're probably nursing a million times a day when your other mama friends are on a set schedule with feedings. It's okay. There will come a day when he is not attached to your boob and you will feel human again. It will get better.

Because I used to have to nurse Dylan so often, I found ways to pass the time. I caught up on Facebook. I watched basketball late at night and tried to learn the lingo so I could talk with Gabe the next day (and so that when I did, it would at least seem like I knew what I was talking about when it came to rebounds and trades). I found that I had a particular liking for LeBron James and was more apt to watch an hour of a Cleveland Cavaliers game than I was to watch a Lifetime movie. I also thought a lot about writing this book, because I couldn't seem to find any support in any of the books that I was reading.

And then I saw her—a blonde girl about my age, running with a jogging stroller behind my house. I had no idea there was another stay-at-home mom in my neighborhood! Hooray, someone who would get it! I had to meet her.

Those next few months became a lifeline. That mystery girl's name was Theresa, and she lived just a few doors down from me. She had a baby boy, Kingston, who was just a few months older than Dylan. We exchanged stories over coffee and watched our boys play while we lamented about the previous night's lack of sleep. We bounced ideas off one another, and we bonded over the fact that both of our boys had reflux. I didn't feel alone anymore, and it was reassuring to know that I wasn't the only one struggling. Life was better, and I'm so grateful to Theresa for being the support that I needed. As it would turn out, I would need her more than I knew then, because reflux was not the end of our problems with Dylan.

It just happened to be the first of many.

3

MOPS

*"Somewhere out there beneath the pale moonlight.
Someone's thinking of me and loving me tonight."*
– James Horner, Barry Mann, *Cynthia Weil from the movie,* An American Tail

Support is such a crucial thing when you are parenting a child with behavioral issues. God was, of course, my center, but I couldn't ignore that I had isolated myself off from others because of time restraints, the sense of judgment, and the feeling of not being able to connect. I needed a change. We aren't islands— we're not meant to go through life alone!

I would say the turning point for me with feeling supported with Dylan was when I started going to MOPS (Mothers of Preschoolers). I was writing for a local magazine and one of my first assignments was to interview a local mothers' group. I had never heard of MOPS before and felt like I needed to experience a meeting (as well as interview the leaders) to write a well-informed article. I went to a meeting to sit in with the group and see what it was all about. Without a doubt, that meeting changed my life—not just as a mother, but as a person. That was the first time I had ever experienced the word of God with other women. I had been going to church, but I hadn't ever heard anything like I heard at MOPS. It was different. It was welcoming. And it was safe.

Monett MOPS Steering Team, my first year as coordinator

My parents were Mormons when they married, and my brother and sister were baptized into the faith. But by the time I was born, my parents were well on their way to a divorce and had left the Mormon religion. God was never brought up in my childhood, and it was all very foreign to me. I felt completely out of my element going to this meeting, but I was interested in learning more about the group—not just because of my writing assignment, but because I was a new mom (Dylan was just over one at the time) and desperate for some advice.

He wasn't sleeping through the night by any means, and I was really nervous about going to the MOPS meeting since I hadn't really been out of the house much with Dylan. I hadn't let anyone watch him. He stayed home with me for the most part, and I was about to leave him in a room at MOPS with MOPPETS volunteers? What the heck were MOPPETS?

I dropped Dylan off in one of the classrooms and placed him in the arms of a very sweet volunteer. A stranger, but a very sweet stranger. I sat down at a table and was immediately welcomed by the woman sitting next to me. She had heard I was coming to interview the group and had made me one of their crafts to take home. I spent the next two hours listening and fellowshipping with other women and by the end, it felt less like work and more like an answer to so many prayers. The truth is, I needed them more than I knew. Shortly after that meeting, I joined MOPS and have been in the group ever since. Six years later, I am now a MOPS Ministry Coach and have made the most amazing friends.

These women pray for me, pray with me, and check in on me when they know I've had an especially hard day or week with Dylan. They celebrate my highs and pick me up during my lows. They accept me for me and they embrace my family as a part of me—including Dylan. I know that might sound simple, but it's really not. It's a big deal to me because I have felt very uncomfortable and very unwanted in many a situation because of the way Dylan behaves. In order for me to bring him anywhere, I have to feel comfortable with the people I'm with. The women in MOPS are those people.

MOPS is also the first place that Dylan started learning about Jesus. He grew up in MOPS and every third Friday of the month, I knew that Dylan would be taught about the Word from volunteers who were grounded in their beliefs. MOPS was the pivotal place for us to start learning about God's love.

After joining various Bible studies, going to church, and hanging up the scripture cards that we made at MOPS, I accepted Jesus Christ as my savior and asked for His forgiveness for my sins. I was baptized in October 2011 and have continued to draw on the Lord for my strength.

My mom continually asks me how I make it through the days that are really bad with Dylan. It's the same answer every time: God. I pray…a lot. Prayer is what gets me through each day and sometimes even minute to minute. I was talking to my mom the other day about the new things we're going through with Dylan, and I could hear the sadness in her voice when she said, "I'm so sorry, Meg." I wasn't sad, though. I felt hopeful. Really hopeful, and I can only chalk that up to being in the presence of the Holy Spirit.

I do worry about Dylan's faith, but I know that it's not my responsibility to show him who God is. It is my responsibility to make sure that I raise him in the church and provide him with the necessary tools to make his own decision about his faith. I try not to harp on him about things, but I do try and pray with him as much as I can about self-control, kindness, and doing what is right. I can tell you a few things that have helped me share Jesus with him:

- MOPS
- Regularly attending church
- Random acts of kindness
- Praying with him, for him, and in front of him
- Scripture cards for kids (see the appendix at the back of book). These were particularly fun when he was in the three-to-four-year-old range and enjoyed holding his own little book, flipping through the pages, and looking at the glossy pictures.
- Songs of praise. I try and play these in the car and in the house. Whether I think at the time that he was listening or not, he'll pop out a tune down the road, and I'll realize that he was.

- A Christian-based school, if it's in the budget. Fortunately, we were able to send Dylan to a private Christian preschool that was attached to our church building. I think this is huge. When the curriculum includes not just math, science, history, and English, but an actual account of Jesus' story...that helps. Unfortunately, we're not able to send Dylan to a private elementary school at this time because of finances, but I do feel like I can see the difference.

- Taking him to the local Christian bookstore and signing up for their birthday club. I did this with all three of my kids and they really enjoy it. Every birthday, Dylan gets a postcard in the mail and gets to come in to the store and pick out a book. This gives us a chance to get a book that we might not otherwise pick up in a mainstream store. It also gives this mama a chance to browse through the Bible studies!

To say that MOPS has played a part in my mothering to Dylan would be a huge understatement. I think it has played one of the most important parts in my parenting to Dylan. It keeps me accountable to things I know are right and gives me the much-needed two hours away each month that makes me a better mom. If you're not in a MOPS group, you need to be, and you can visit www.mops.org for more information.

With the confidence I was gaining from being around other moms who accepted me, I felt strong enough to venture out of our little bubble. I started looking around for other things that Dylan and I could do together, and one of those very first things was Itsy Bitsy Yoga.

4

He's a Scooter

"Speed doesn't matter. Forward is forward."
– Anonymous

I had been taking Dylan to Itsy Bitsy Yoga once a week and had made a great group of friends who all had babies the same age. Things were fun for a while, but I soon noticed that Dylan wasn't taking the same steps as the other kids—in fact, he wasn't taking any steps. He sat up in yoga for the first time at seven months... okay, good. But when the yoga teacher started flipping Bilibos over to make a caterpillar for the kids to walk on, Dylan was the only one not walking (side note for those of you who might not know what a Bilibo is—it's okay. I didn't know what they were either until this yoga class. See the Appendix in this book for an explanation of what they are!). I thought, okay, he's not walking yet, no biggee. The problem was, Dylan showed no interest in walking at all. In fact, he wasn't even crawling! He was scooting. On his butt. Sure it was cute at first, and I still think of it as being cute when I picture him doing it in my mind, but what wasn't cute were the stares from other moms who would say things like, "Oh my gosh! Look at that! I've never seen anything like that before."

So, right off the bat, my child is not a monkey. He is not a *thing*. He just so happens to be getting around differently than your child. I started to feel so bad about the way people were looking at him that I became insecure. I stopped taking him to yoga and went back to the pediatrician to find out why, at fifteen months, he was still not crawling or walking, but scooting.

My pediatrician recommended we find a physical therapist to work with Dylan on building muscle tone to help him start walking. I was puzzled. Muscle tone? Why wouldn't my baby have proper muscle tone? That's when we were referred to a neurologist. Let me just tell you, that was probably one of the worst days of my life.

My husband is an audiologist, and though I'm thankful for his job, there are negative sides to him seeing patients. He can't call in sick or just go in late. He has patients with set appointments who are expecting him to be there. So I ended up going to a lot of appointments by myself, this one included.

There was a bright yellow line down the middle of the stark white floor in the neurologist's office—we'll call him Dr. A. When Dr. A came in, he asked me a few questions and then swiftly picked Dylan up out of my arms, snatched off Dylan's shoes, and put Dylan down on one end of the line. I think my mouth was still hanging down to the floor at the way he grabbed Dylan from me when he said, "Hmm. He'll definitely never be an athlete, and he probably won't play sports in school."

I was in shock, but Dr. A wasn't done. "I think we should run some tests to see if he has some sort of muscle deficiency," he said.

By the end of the visit, what I came away hearing was "I think your son has muscular dystrophy (MD)," so that's what I relayed to Gabe on the phone. What was actually said was, "We can rule out MD," but he did recommend doing a muscle biopsy to see if there was some sort of gene mutation. Now, moms out there, I used to beat myself up about this. How could I have heard wrong? How could I have gotten MD confused with muscle biopsy? How could I have scared my husband like that?

Have you found yourself in a similar situation? If so, stop beating yourself up! The truth is, I'm not a doctor and I don't know what all of this stuff means. Most of you probably don't, either. When we hear a lot of these words for the first time, we're usually overwhelmed, under-slept, and just trying to do the best we can. Give yourself a break and, most of all, give yourself some grace to be human.

Gabe tells me now that was the worst day of his life, and I still regret that I was responsible for it. Thankfully, he has learned to love my little quirks and knows that if there is ever a crucial doctor's appointment, he needs to go with me because I get overwhelmed. But I couldn't just rely on Gabe. I wanted to be an advocate for my son, so I developed some ways that I could help myself cope. I hope they help you too.

- **Write out your questions ahead of time.**
- **Don't be afraid to ask your questions.** Take notes at the appointment. If the doctor doesn't ask you if you have any questions, tell him you have some you'd like to ask. Sadly, a lot of these doctors rush you in and out. Don't let them. Take your time. Don't leave that office until you feel confident that you understand what they're telling you.
- **Ask for printouts.** Our pediatrician's office started doing this, and it was really helpful for me to look back at and reread.

- **Do your research.** Find out as much as you can about your child's doctor. Google became a fast friend of mine. Why is this important? Well, if I'm going to trust what this doctor tells me about my child's health and well-being, I need to know that he is qualified to do so. For example, which I will explain later on in this book when we get to the section about ADHD, one of my son's neurologists had a reputation in the medical field as being a pill pusher. How did I find this out? By talking to other medical professionals. What did I do about it? Looked outside of our network for a neurologist who had a good reputation.

- **Pray.** Sadly, I didn't know how to do this until much later on in Dylan's life. But the good news is, it's never too late to pray.

- **Get support.** Call a friend, family member, or your spouse before and after the appointment. Having accountability with someone you trust can make all the difference in your attitude.

After the news of Dylan's muscular situation, we enrolled in a state program called First Steps. At the time, we were living in Missouri and found out there was a way we could get Dylan's physical therapy at home, instead of driving forty-five minutes away and paying a seventy-five dollar co-pay for thirty minutes at a time. Yes, crazy inconvenient AND expensive. But when you think there might be a chance your child can't walk, you'll do just about anything to make sure he does.

Martha was Dylan's physical therapist, and she couldn't have been a more perfect fit for our family. We happened to live across the street from a rehabilitation center where she worked. Dylan was seventeen months old when we started physical therapy in the spring of 2010. She came to our house once a week, sometimes twice a week, and eventually once a month when Dylan started walking. He took his first steps at twenty months.

I learned a lot during those weekly, two-hour physical therapy sessions with Martha. I watched as she marched around our kitchen table and encouraged Dylan to do the same. I was surprised when she told me she wanted to teach Dylan how to crawl first, because it was an important part of his brain's development.

Gabe helping Dylan walk for one of the very first times.
We learned this trick from his physical therapist.

Each new milestone came after hours and hours of hard work. Martha would draw a line down our driveway with a piece of chalk and hold Dylan's hands while she walked backward, guiding him to follow. I watched her blow bubbles for Dylan so she could entice him to jump and pop one. She gave me tips like lining cereal boxes up in my house and letting Dylan kick them down to help him work on balance.

Sometimes she would meet us at the park and hold Dylan's hand as he tried to walk up the steps to the slide. We talked through all of these sessions, but she always had her eyes on Dylan and gave me hope that he would be just fine.

I look back at that year and realize how much I isolated myself from others at times. I was slightly embarrassed that Dylan wasn't walking, and I found myself not having much in common with other moms during play dates because I was in such a different season with Dylan. I was focused on right, left, right, left, up and down the stairs, while my friends were telling me about their kids kicking a ball and running. It wasn't their fault. It wasn't mine. I just didn't know how to relate to them when my whole world was full of doctors' visits and not knowing what Dylan's future would look like. Martha was part of my support then, and I'm so grateful that she came into our lives.

Gabe and I made the decision to not have the muscle biopsy done. We were told that it was an extremely painful procedure, especially for a child. No matter the results, it wouldn't change our course of treatment for Dylan. By this time, he was still in physical therapy and doing great. Slow progress, but still progress. We felt like if there was no benefit from having the biopsy done, than why put him through the pain? It turns out we made the right decision. Dylan started walking. We had our follow up at Dr. A's office, and he was released from his care with a medical note in his file: benign delay—basically, your child walked late and we don't know why.

It's a sad fact that not every family is able to pay for physical therapy, especially when it's our children that desperately need it. I encourage you to look into any assistance that you can find. Speak to your doctors about state or government programs. Research yourself. And if all else fails, research techniques that you can practice at home. But above all, never give up on searching for help.

24

5

Disciplining an Out-of-Control Child

(well...trying to)

"You gotta get up and try and try again."
- PINK

After Dylan learned to walk, it felt, for a while, like we were in the clear. The next few years went on as most toddler years do. However, as much as we thought we were out of the woods, along came another issue with Dylan—his tantrums. Now all children have tantrums at some point or another. They're tiny people learning to control their emotions, and breakdowns are bound to happen along the way. But what I started to realize with Dylan was that the amount of time he spent crying, yelling, and throwing himself around probably wasn't normal.

I won't lie. I'd seen the writing on the wall and already had my suspicions, but I had hoped that I was being overprotective or even a bit dramatic. It also didn't help that Gabe was in complete denial. Every time I would try and talk to him about Dylan, he would tell me that I was overreacting and everything was fine. I started to believe that maybe I was going crazy. Maybe I was making too big a deal out of Dylan's behavior, and it really wasn't that bad. I used to run circles in my head, day in and day out, trying to decide if what I was witnessing was normal. Since I was the one home with Dylan while Gabe was at work, I saw his quirks and mannerisms that Gabe wasn't always privy to seeing. Don't get me wrong; he did see them, but just not to the degree or as often as I did.

But I knew. I knew in my heart that once again, something wasn't right. Each time I mentioned it to the pediatrician, she would ask me a new question or tell me to try this or wait until he's this old. But nothing worked. She also asked me (as did every other specialist) if my son was fascinated with spinning objects and/or would he stare at them for endless amounts of time? I learned later that this is a very typical question when diagnosing a child with autism. My answer was always no and inside, I kept telling myself, okay, well it's not that bad if he doesn't do that. He may have tantrums but at least he doesn't watch spinning objects all day.

I tried 1-2-3 Magic Parenting, Love & Logic Parenting, spanking, time-outs, taking his toys away, loss of privileges, less TV time, getting on his level and explaining to him that it's not okay to scream for that long and that loud—you name it, I tried it.

Then things started to get scary when Dylan started trying to hurt himself. Did other two and three year olds scrape their fingernails down their face until they drew blood? I was thinking, probably not. He used to throw things in his room when I made him go to time out. I was worried that he might climb the bookcase and topple it onto himself, or rip the wand off the blinds and poke his eye out. Therapists told me to take everything out of his room. Everything.

"Make it so he can't hurt himself," they'd say. Okay, well, how do I take his hands from him? How do I get him to not scratch himself?

"Hold him in a bear hug, like this," they'd say. Okay, what do I do when he starts biting me, kicking me, and spitting at me?

"Well, is there any abuse going on at home?"

That one stopped me cold.

"Often times, children who have been abused will lash out like this," I was told. "We see this in kids who have been adopted too. It's called reattachment parenting. Does Dylan go to daycare? Has he been out of your sight?"

"No, no, and no." Absolutely NOT.

Now, you're probably thinking what I was thinking: our poor family! First he has reflux, then he can't walk, and now behavioral issues?

So we started with a basic child therapist. She was short-lived, though, because, ironically, she didn't really like kids. Pick another profession, maybe?

I remember taking Dylan to one of his sessions with this doctor. I sat on the old, ripped couch while she sat across from me. Dylan played on the floor with some toys, and she and I talked about what brought me in that day. "Don't do that," she'd bark at Dylan.

"You need to be gentle with those toys," she'd say shortly thereafter. "These are my personal toys from home. Be careful with them." Ummm, lady, do you know why we're here? My son has severe behavioral issues, so your precious toys are probably not the best thing for him to play with, if you want him to play nicely. Just a thought.

I can't remember how many times we saw her, but it wasn't many. I felt like a bad mom already but was amazed at how much worse I felt after talking with her. "What forms of discipline, if any, do you use with Dylan?" she asked.

"We spank. But that doesn't work. So, we mainly put him in time-out. We've tried Love & Logic Parenting, 1-2-3 Magic Parenting, and nothing is working," I explained.

"How often does he go to time-out?" she asked. "And where do you put him for time-out?"

"He sometimes goes to his room, but he started destroying things, so we moved him to the laundry room. It's the only room in our house with a door where he cannot throw anything."

"Okay, and how often is that?" she asked, still looking down at her notepad.

"A lot," I stated. "He throws a tantrum for most of the day, so he's in there a lot."

She proceeded to tell me that this was extremely harmful to Dylan and time-outs are to be used only in the most severe situations, for only a few minutes at a time. What I was doing was not right and could affect Dylan's well-being. I left her office that day feeling like I wanted to jump off a cliff.

I knew, of course, that no one should put their child in time-out for most of the day, but what, then, was a parent supposed to do with a child who screamed, yelled, hit, bit, kicked, and misbehaved most of the day? I felt like I was in a lose-lose situation with no right answer.

28

It took me a while to "recover" from that therapy session. The fact that I can still remember most of what we talked about that day should tell you how awful I felt at that moment, so we stopped seeing that therapist and started looking for another.

As someone who has gone to therapy most of her life, I get that there is supposed to be a good "fit" with your therapist. You kind of just know when things jive and you feel like this person can help you in some way. I didn't feel that way with this woman. I felt like she was judging me and basically calling me an unfit mother. I didn't need another person telling me that I was failing when I already felt that way inside.

But she wasn't all bad because she gave us a great piece of advice: "I think Dylan has anxiety," she told me.

Why would Dylan have anxiety? He's three, I thought. What does he have to be anxious about? But I took her advice and tried to make the home as soothing and stress-free as possible. Instead of spanking or doing time-outs, I knelt down, eye-to-eye, and tried to reason with a three-year-old who had just screamed for more than half the day. It was ridiculous. You can't reason with three-year-olds. I know that now, but his therapist had me feeling so bad about putting Dylan in time-out that I'd actually stopped, and after that, he was officially calling the shots in my house.

Gabe and I were also fighting a lot. Simply put, I thought there was something wrong with Dylan and he did not. I thought there was some sort of chemical imbalance that was causing Dylan to act the way that he was acting because I just knew this could not be how other children behaved. But when Gabe didn't see it (or wouldn't see it, maybe), I questioned my parenting, telling myself that I was too emotional about his outbursts. I'd say, "Meg, pull it together. He's three and you're the adult. You've got this."

But I didn't have it.

We rarely ventured out due to Dylan's sporadic outbursts, but we did decide to visit my brother in Texas during the winter of 2010. On our way home, we stopped in Oklahoma City and rented a hotel room. The next morning, as we were packing up and getting dressed, I attempted to put Dylan's winter coat on. Now, you must know, Dylan has never liked it when the seasons change. He does not like going from shorts to pants or from T-shirts to long sleeve shirts. It just isn't his thing, because he gets overwhelmed with all sorts of sensory issues from the change. However, it was the middle of winter and it was freezing, so I was not going to let up on the coat.

I kept trying to get it on him while he wriggled and squirmed away, and he screamed the entire time. In fact, as we walked down the hallway from our room to the elevator, an elderly man opened his door. "What's going on?" he asked.

"Oh, nothing," Gabe explained. "Our son just doesn't want to wear his coat."

"It sounds like a lot more than that to me," said the man. "It sounds like there might be some child abuse going on."

Gabe and I just looked at each other in sheer shock. What? Child abuse? In that moment, we were genuinely offended because it was so far from the truth, and we were so horrified that we would be accused of hurting our son. Gabe puffed his chest out a little bit bigger, and I swear he grew ten inches when he started to give this man a piece of his mind.

Through their arguing back and forth, this man threatened to call the police on us because he was sure there was child abuse. I'll never forget what Gabe said back to him. "Go ahead and call the police. Tell them I'll meet them downstairs at the front desk, and I'll let them know that you called them all the way out here because my son wouldn't put his coat on."

We eventually got in the elevator. I was shaking and could not believe what had just happened. I was sad, mad, frustrated, embarrassed, a ball of emotions—you name it, I was feeling it. But as upset as we were, it finally hit Gabe—this was the magnitude of Dylan's tantrums, that a stranger genuinely thought we were hurting our child to the point that he would risk his safety by stepping in.

Today I can appreciate the gesture as being the brave thing for this elderly gentleman to do. He was wrong about the abuse, of course, but it was still writing on the wall as far as Dylan's behavior was concerned. In that moment, we both knew that we couldn't continue living this way.

PCIT

"When you are a mother, you are never really alone in your thoughts. A mother always has to think twice, once for herself and once for her child."

– Sophia Loren

Our next therapist was actually for all three of us. By then, we'd had another child, Hannah, and I was pregnant with my third. It was the summer before Dylan started his second year of preschool, and things had gotten worse. Dylan would not talk to me, did not want to be around me, and seemed, by all accounts, to hate me. We were told he might have oppositional defiant disorder (ODD).

I've compiled a list of six behavioral signs to look out for if you suspect that your child might have ODD. If you and your child are at odds more than you are at peace, it may be time to seek professional help. Early intervention can help you and your child get through the tough times and give you the answers you so desperately need.

- **Tantrums** - tantrums that last hours and hours over absolutely nothing. Throwing, hitting, spitting, crying, screaming, and yelling with no end in sight.

- **Defiant Behavior** - doing the exact opposite of what is asked, whether it is something small like brushing their teeth or something big like not hitting.

- **Mood Swings** - one minute your child is happy and laughing, and the next he's grumpy and mad. This could be over something as minute as a toy not working the way he wants it to.

- **Lack of Sleep** - interrupted sleep can only add to an already explosive child.

- **Praise** - children with ODD don't always like praise. If this is the case in your situation, find something that she does like, such as imitating play.

- **Lack of Affection** - children with ODD don't always show affection. Try not to make a big deal about it and just move on. Relish the moments when he does give you a hug, and remember that some kids ask for love in the most unloving ways.

Most importantly, hang in there. Don't be too hard on yourself as the parent, and give yourself a break when you need it. Having a child with ODD is extremely difficult and can feel very isolating.

In order to combat this new diagnosis, we enrolled in a sixteen-week therapy program called Parent-Child Interaction Therapy (PCIT) with a doctor who specialized in the program. The difference between this therapy and traditional therapies is that this one practices behavioral relationships between the parent and child while in the presence of a doctor. Instead of being at an appointment where you are encouraged to go home and practice this learned behavior, the idea behind PCIT is that there is live, ongoing treatment and coaching.

The three of us went every single week for one-hour sessions and learned how to re-parent Dylan. I would stand on one side of the glass with an earpiece in my ear, and I would play with Dylan while Gabe and the doctor stood on the other side of the glass in a different room. They could see me, but I couldn't see them. The doctor talked to me through the earpiece and would coach me through the parent-child interaction process. Once my time was up, it would be Gabe's turn, and so on.

There were times where I felt like the tools we learned in PCIT actually worked, but at the end of the sixteen weeks, I didn't feel any closer to figuring out what was wrong with Dylan. He was still throwing tantrums. He was still defiant. He seemed to manipulate every situation he was in, and our family life was still really difficult having him in it. Mind you, we had a wonderful set of friends from church who we asked to watch Hannah while we went to these weekly therapy sessions, but even this was hard on me since I knew I was taking time away from her for yet another situation with Dylan.

We had homework every day, which consisted of filling out a one-page form after playing with Dylan for fifteen minutes, several times a day. During these playtimes, we would pick three different toys and take them into a room in the house where it was completely quiet so that Dylan and I, or Dylan and Gabe, could focus on uninterrupted play. The point of the homework was to allow Dylan to control the play environment and let him choose which toy he wanted to play with out of those three. This is called Child-Directed Interaction (CDI). We were to let him lead the playtime and only redirect him with positive language should he start doing something we didn't want him to do. For example, if Dylan started throwing one of the toys, I was to say something like, "Dylan, I really liked it when you were playing nicely with that toy," and not say something like, "Dylan, stop throwing the toy."

You may be laughing at this example, and I don't blame you

because, as I'm typing it, I'm thinking how ridiculous it sounds. But, when you have a child who is as difficult as Dylan and you deal with it on a daily basis, you are willing to try anything.

Gabe and I were both on board and willing to do whatever the doctor told us to do. When she gave us homework every week, we were even kind of excited, because it was something no doctor had ever done before. We thought, "Okay, maybe this is the answer! Maybe we just needed to change our parenting style to accommodate Dylan."

The acronyms PDI (Parent-Directed Interaction) and CDI (Child-Directed Interaction) became our new language that year. One of our homework assignments was to read about and learn the language we would need to know during CDI and PDI. CDI works on building the relationship between the child and the parent(s), and PDI focuses on the discipline side of things. Since we couldn't have the paper in front of us during the actual session each week, we had to try and memorize it. The doctor was always there to talk to us and guide us during playtime in our earpiece, but it was hard to always say and do the right thing. I was so afraid that I would mess Dylan up during playtime or I would ruin the session.

There's an acronym used in PCIT called "P.R.I.D.E." and it stands for, "Praise, Reflection, Imitate, Description, and Enjoyment." Each letter represented something Gabe and I needed to do during every playtime with Dylan. If we did these things, we were told, Dylan's behavior would improve, and the opposition we experienced almost every moment of every day would get better! So, just imagine the guilt I felt when it didn't work.

The first letter is "P" for praise. If Dylan was playing with blocks and stacking them up nicely, I would say something like,

"Dylan, I really like how you're playing nicely with those blocks. I love that tower you're building." Now, sometimes Dylan would smile and continue playing like the handbook says a child should do, but sometimes he would purposely throw a block or knock his tower down after I praised him. Almost always, whenever I praised Dylan, he would end up doing something to upset me. It was always the opposite behavior of what the doctor told me should happen.

The second letter, "R," reflects what your child is doing. Think of a mirror. You say back whatever your child is playing with, exhibiting, etc. If Dylan was playing with farm animals and he was making animal noises to show that cow was mooing or the pig was oinking, I would say something like, "Oink, oink! I like when you make the pig oink, Dylan." Dylan would usually just look at me with this puzzled expression and I can only imagine what he was thinking...my mom is crazy.

The third letter, "I," was for imitating. If Dylan was racing a car on the table, I would race a car on the table. This was supposed to show that I was watching what he was doing, and I was paying attention to detail with how he was playing. I was imitating his play. Most of the time, Dylan would do something he wasn't supposed to, like throw the car, just to see if I would imitate that. It was during those moments in PCIT that I knew we were dealing with a very smart child. "He's on to this," I'd tell Gabe. "He's totally playing us."

The fourth letter, "D," was for behavior description. I would watch what Dylan was playing with and explain word for word what he was doing. The doctor gave us a great tip, which was to think of this one as a radio announcer, a play-by-play of what was going on. "Dylan is putting the blocks in the bucket, and he's organizing them by color. Oh, wait, he just took a block out and put the lid on the container. Oh, never mind, he put that block back in the container and now he's closing the container." We got quite a few laughs out of this one. It was fun to see Dylan get happy when he knew that his dad and I were completely focused on him. Sometimes he was annoyed, but sometimes I could tell that he was totally soaking it up.

The fifth and last letter was "E" for enjoyment. "Dylan, I really like how you put that guy in that blue car. He looks like he's having fun!"

During CDI therapy, Gabe and I were scored on how many times we exhibited each letter of PRIDE. At the end of each playtime, the doctor would go over how we did and where we could improve. For example, this is what some of our results looked like:

Ruffing Family

Mom	1st	2nd
Behavioral Description	4	12
Reflection	9	5
Labeled Praise	5	7

Dad	1st	2nd
Behavioral Description	0	3
Reflection	8	19
Labeled Praise	3	8

Looks confusing, right? I know. When you break it down, though, it's really quite neat what you gather from your parenting style. You'll see that during my first CDI time with Dylan, there were four times when I described what he was doing. In the second CDI, I got all the way up to twelve with the help of the doctor coaching me in my ear.

While Gabe excelled in the reflection stage of CDI, he needed to improve in his behavioral description. We took these results from each session and talked about them with the doctor and in the car together. Sometimes we laughed about how poorly we did in one area and praised each other when we did well. I'd like to think Gabe and I learned some neat things about each other during this time. We were able to pinpoint our strengths and weaknesses in parenting, which most people don't get to do. But while this can be extremely helpful, it can also be an area of vulnerability.

I mentioned earlier that I struggled with guilt during this time. I felt guilty about having to leave Hannah during these appointments. I felt guilty having to take Dylan to these therapy sessions every week. I felt guilty about having a child who needed so much medical intervention that it was affecting my marriage. I also had a hard time processing some of the CDI scores and would mentally beat myself up about how good or bad I thought I was acting as Dylan's mom. Although I knew it wasn't healthy for my marriage or me, I let these feelings consume me and direct my days before the sun even rose. I knew I needed to see a therapist on my own, but I wondered how I could ever find the time.

There are many things I look back on during my early years with Dylan that I regret. One of the biggest things is not taking better care of myself. However, we do what we know and what I knew was that I needed to survive. I just wanted to make it through those tough years and pray that I would come out alive at the other end. PCIT was that hope for me, and I prayed it would be the answer to Dylan's problems.

Unfortunately, while the idea behind this type of therapy is very clever, it didn't seem to work with Dylan. There was no rhyme or reason to his behavior during playtime and the rules we were to follow during PDI and CDI at home never worked 100 percent of the time. I remember telling Gabe on many occasions that I felt like Dylan was immune to therapy. What was supposed to work for other children was only working part time on my child, and there was never any way to predict which outcome he would display.

There were times when we felt like it was working. There were times when PCIT seemed to be the answer. But by the end of the program, his doctor said, "Well, I'm not really sure if this is what Dylan has. I think he might do better with an occupational therapist (OT)."

Talk about feeling deflated! When we enrolled in PCIT, I thought this program would work wonders for us, and I was crushed when it didn't. Still, even though it wasn't a success for us, I don't want to discourage you from trying PCIT if you think it could work for your family. Personally, I think it's a great resource for those families truly dealing with oppositionally defiant children. No matter what you choose, let me encourage you to please keep going with some sort of behavior treatment. I still learned some neat tips from this program that I continue to use today, and you will too, even if therapy isn't the complete success you hope for.

After PCIT, we were referred to an OT who was in the same building, with the same clinic, just on the third floor.

The third floor which is also known as the Autism Center floor. The words are right there in front of you when you walk out of the elevator. When I saw them, I held back the tears. Dylan doesn't have autism, I thought. Or at least, I don't think he has autism.

Or did he have autism, but his PCIT doctor just didn't want to tell me?

7

OT

*"It's been a terrible, horrible, no good, very bad day.
My mom says some days are like that."*
– *Judith Viorst in* Alexander and the Terrible, Horrible,
No Good, Very Bad Day

After PCIT was over, we were referred to Amy Vaughan, an occupational therapist who helps children with sensory issues. Since the majority of Dylan's tantrums seemed to stem from things not feeling "right," we already felt like he had some sensory issues. It could be the way his shoes fit, his pants, his shirt…anything, really. His socks could bother him one day and not the next. Haircuts were impossible, and we had to do the best we could at home. But often, there didn't seem to be a pattern as to what didn't feel right. When we did find something that Dylan would tolerate wearing, we always bought two pairs.

He has always been sensitive to tags in shirts. When you have a child who has sensory issues, you find ways to make them feel more comfortable. Gabe was really good at finding tagless, stylish shirts from Under Armor. Dylan looked really cute in his sporty shirts, and it seemed to be a win-win for everyone.

Pants have always been a tough one, and I think I've seen Dylan wear jeans once in his life. He usually wears athletic pants or shorts, but again, we were able to find ones that worked. However, what seemed to bother him the most was the elastic band around the waist. He would constantly bend down, jump up, and then fall to the ground screaming. He would twist at the waistband and scream, "It doesn't feel right!" It was nearly impossible to get Dylan to calm down during these episodes, so they usually ended with him taking off all his clothes or continuing with the tantrum as we proceeded with whatever we were doing at the time.

Underwear has never been something that Dylan could tolerate. We've tried everything. At first, I thought, "Wow, what kind of mom am I that I would let my kindergartener go to school without underwear?" I even got a call from his school one day, with the school nurse telling me I needed to get over there and bring my son a change of clothes because he'd had an accident. "An accident," I thought? "And bring some underwear, please," she said.

I got to the school and had no idea what was going on. I saw Dylan who looked really embarrassed. "What's going on buddy?" I asked.

"Nothing. I just have a little smudge in my pants," he said.

"A smudge? What do you mean?" I asked.

"Mom, it's nothing. Just give me my pants," he pleaded.

I helped him change and told him it was okay. "It's no big deal," I said. "This happens to people all the time."

"Really?" he asked. "Like who?"

"Well, when I was your age, I was waiting for the bus at school. I remember standing in line and I had to pee really bad. I ended up peeing right there, and because the sidewalk slanted down, my pee ran all the way down through everyone's feet. It was so embarrassing."

"Really?" he laughed.

"Yeah, really," I said. "And I had to have my dad come pick me up. He showed up with a towel and picked me up and put me in the car. I know it's embarrassing, Dylan, but it'll be okay."

Dylan walked back to his classroom, and the nurse asked me if I'd brought him new underwear. I politely explained that Dylan had sensory issues and underwear just wasn't his thing. I was used to (and still am) getting strange looks from people about his fuss over clothes. I chose to end the situation with a simple thank you and walked out.

I still get strange looks, but Dr. Lucy Jane Miller, author of *Sensational Kids*, says that as many as one in twenty children in the United States have SPD (Sensory Processing Disorder). It also usually manifests in a more intense way because children don't always have the right words to express themselves. Of course, this realization took me a long time to figure out and accept, but with the knowledge I gained from going to OT with Dylan and joining an online support group for families with SPD, I was able to become a bit more educated.

Sadly enough, though, I don't think there are many excellent resources out there book-wise for SPD. I can tell you that I was able to take bits of information from Carol Kranowitz's, *The Out-of-Sync Child: Recognizing and Coping with Sensory Integration Dysfunction*. My problem with this one is that it was written in 1998.

That's almost twenty years ago! Amy Vaughan's book, *Positively Sensory! A Guide to Help Your Child Develop Positive Approaches to Learning and Cope with Sensory Processing Difficulty* is the book you need to get if you are looking for practical tips and advice on how to help your child. I wish this book had been written when we first learned of Dylan's sensory challenges, because it's written in a way that is easy to understand for parents with less medical jargon than many other SPD books.

SPD is not officially included in the *Diagnostic and Statistical Manual of Mental Disorders* (DSM), but it is considered to be a subsidiary dysfunction of other disorders like ADHD, Asperger's, etc. and is coded under such diagnoses to ensure insurance coverage. If a disorder is not recognized, insurance does not cover it. Although this book can be intimidating just on the sheer presence of its massive size, I encourage you to look at it. Read about the different disorders, and it will make you feel like you have taken back some of the control you might have lost when you didn't know what was going on with your child. However, it will probably make you sad too. I had a hard time reading about different diagnoses because they sounded all too familiar with what Dylan was exhibiting behavior-wise. The material came as a real smack-in-the-face moment, and at that point I knew I had to accept that Dylan was different from other kids.

You're probably thinking, "What's wrong with being different than other kids? Doesn't she love her kid?"

Well, of course I love him! I wouldn't trade Dylan for any other kid in the whole world, even on his worst days. I learned in my own personal therapy that I had to let go of the child I thought Dylan should be and start accepting the child that he was. I also had to stop feeling so guilty about thinking Dylan should be any other way than how he was born. The truth is that we all want our kids to be normal.

We all want them to succeed as individuals and to help create a life for them that is easy, fun, and rewarding. And I still think things can be that way for these kids if we have a better understanding of how they're wired. That's why I'm writing this book, for the other families out there that want and need information, support, and just a simple how-to book on making it through the day with their children.

Now, back to Dr. Vaughan—first of all, I think she's amazing. Talk about someone who really loves her job and enjoys working with children! She was a breath of fresh air after having been with so many professionals who seemed tired and burned out. I was a tired parent and grasping at straws for answers, and she really raised the bar and helped me feel like I could take back some sort of control with Dylan.

I remember our first meeting with her. I was literally shaking on the inside. I was so full of hope, questions, fear, excitement, and just the feeling of the things unknown. Could she help us live normal lives?

Dr. Vaughan went through Dylan's history at that first meeting and had Dylan do things like kneel on the floor or stack blocks. This was an assessment to see where he was at with his motor and sensory processing skills, and to determine what kind of treatment plan would be best for him.

We saw Dr. Vaughan every two weeks and worked on different gross motor skills. Because Dylan didn't have great balance, she worked with him on things like standing on one foot, or having both of his feet off the ground (balance while sitting in a swing without support/gravitational insecurity responses is the technical explanation). He seemed to enjoy OT, and I was really good about taking the doctor's advice back home and using the techniques she taught me in session.

I would wrap Dylan up like a burrito by laying him on a blanket, rolling it up tight with only his head and feet sticking out, and apply pressure to his pressure points—feet, calves, thighs, hands, arms, and top of the head. The idea was to help calm him and allow him to be present in the moment—helping him feel all of his senses and bring him to a state of relaxation. It worked for a short while. This exercise and many others were part of what OTs call a "sensory diet," though the actual term came from an OT by the name of Patricia Wilbarger (you may have heard about the Wilbarger Brushing Method). It's basically an individualized sensory plan for your child. Since there are different types of sensory processing disorders (some children hate touch, some children can't get enough touch, and some children don't feel touch), each plan is tailored to fit the needs of your child.

For example, I know that chewing gum helps Dylan when he's feeling anxious. I know that the chewing, chomping down, and texture of the gum brings him back to a feeling of control. He is focused on chewing the gum, rather than the situation he's in.

I also know that a rice bucket or Play-Doh will help him when he's super hyper. I can't recall a time when Dylan has ever said "no" to play with either of those things when I've asked him. He could be in the middle of an all-out tantrum, and I could walk over and hold him and say, "Do you want your rice bucket?"

The rice bucket is something that's just for him, and it brings him so much peace. He usually stands at the table and hides small army men or rocks in the grains, and then he slips his hands through them like sand at the beach. Once he's had enough, he puts it away and asks me if he can go outside, watch TV, or so on. But it's a fix for his individual need, which is what a sensory diet tries to focus on.

A sensory diet might look something like this. The Problem Areas are examples of what might set Dylan off. The Individual Solutions are things we use to counter the Problem Area.

Problem Areas	Individual Solution
Fidgets in seat / can't sit still	If he can't sit still, we give him a rice bucket, Play-Doh, or moon sand.
Anxious	If he seems anxious about something, I give him a piece of gum.
Aggressive	When he's aggressive, running around, or amped up, I let him do heavy work such as carrying the laundry basket full of clothes, pushing a wheelbarrow outside, or carrying books up and down the stairs for me. The actual weight of the items helps him handle his emotions and allows him to feel the heaviness of the objects.
Makes humming noises when amped up	When he's humming or making noises that, let's be honest, are extremely annoying to others, I give him a piece of gum or redirect his attention to something else. I have found that if I bring attention to it, he will only do it more. I might say something like, "Dylan, let's go make cookies," or, "Dylan, let's go play outside."
Clothes don't feel right	When his clothes don't feel right, I try to distract him or give him an option between two items. For example, "Dylan you can wear this shirt or that shirt and then we are going to get the mail."

A sensory diet can really help your child cope with the outside world or even just living at home. I have found that it's extremely important to include this in our everyday life with Dylan. It has become part of our routine and is something that I recommend if you're struggling with a day-to-day functional life.

Problem Areas	Individual Solution

Another life saver, and I do mean LIFE SAVER, is telling Dylan the plan for the day. Every day he wakes up and while he's eating breakfast, I say, "Dylan, do you want to hear the plan for today?" If for some reason I have ever forgotten to ask that, you can be sure that Dylan will say, "Mom, what's the plan for today?"

Having a routine is crucial for children like Dylan. He knows what to expect and he knows what the plan is. Of course, like anything, plans can change. My advice to you would be to prepare your child for the change. If you had originally planned to go to the park, but can't now because your dog is sick and needs to go to the vet, you can't expect your child with SPD, anxiety, and so on, to accept that. To set them up for success, you must stick to a plan and say something like, "Honey, because Bailey is sick, I have to take her to the vet. We'll go to the park after that." Or if you can't make it to the park that day, "We'll stay an extra twenty minutes at the park tomorrow since we won't be able to make it today."

I know this probably sounds a lot like catering to your child, or being too indulgent. But this is what I mean when I say that SPD is real. I know, because my child has it. You aren't coddling. You aren't spoiling. You aren't being too indulgent. What you are doing is setting your child up to succeed whenever possible. And I know these things work because I've done them. I've done the research, and I've even veered from these suggestions to see what would happen. The results were exactly what I didn't want: an awful, day-to-day life of barely getting by with my son. These techniques help Dylan enjoy his life so much more, and that makes my life better too.

As I said, I could see a lot of the exercises working for Dylan to help calm him down. I think he liked OT because he got to swing from a seat hanging from the ceiling and lay on his tummy while being pulled like Superman around the third floor. But after several months of therapy, Dylan started to show his true colors. I remember it very clearly: I, Dylan, and Dr. Vaughan were sitting on the floor in one of the OT rooms playing with instruments. We were each taking a turn with an instrument, and Dylan kept going out of turn. On purpose. Because he could. The techniques that once worked with him were no longer working. He was completely manipulating the situation, and he knew it and enjoyed it. Dr. Vaughan looked at me and said, "You know, I really think he could benefit from seeing a child therapist who specializes in play therapy." So, on to the next therapist we went.

The first time we met with Angela Couch at the counseling center, I met with her just one-on-one. Each time after that, I waited in the waiting room with Hannah while Dylan went with Dr. Couch. We did this for several weeks and saw no results. Dylan was not opening up during play therapy, and Dr. Couch wasn't learning anything from the sessions. That's when we heard, "I really think Dylan would benefit from having a psychological evaluation."

Oh, so surprising. Another doctor. But the wait list for the test was a long one, so all we could do was put our names down with the idea that we'd do more research about the testing while we were waiting. Six months later, we took Dylan in for a psych evaluation.

I need to back up a minute here and tell you the biggest reason why we stopped seeing Dr. Couch. It was because she was late for every single one of Dylan's appointments. I'm not talking five minutes. I'm talking thirty to forty minutes, or sometimes even an hour, with no notice. I don't say this to be rude or insulting, but remember, when you're living with a child who has behavior issues, routine is everything. We all know that sometimes things come up, but you should not be with a doctor who continually makes you wait at each appointment, only adding to an already stressful situation. If Dylan is going to be at his best and have his therapy sessions help him, he has to have doctors that understand his need for scheduling and work with him on that. Otherwise, we're starting behind at every appointment before we've even begun!

I remember vividly the day we stopped seeing Dr. Couch, because it was one of many where I just broke down. One thing you'll learn in this journey of parenting a child with severe behavioral issues is that though each day is a struggle, there are some days that are far worse than you could have ever imagined. There are days when medical professionals will let you down and you will lose hope. This was one of those days. We had driven forty-five minutes to Dylan's counseling appointment, only to sit there for another forty-five minutes and still not be seen. I left the office and took Dylan to the mall play area because I felt so guilty that I had dragged him all the way there and, so far, the day had been nothing but awful for him. I remember watching him in the play area when my phone rang. It was Dr. Couch calling to apologize.

I called Gabe afterwards, like I have so many times, and just vented. We took a break from seeing any doctors and therapists while we waited for the psych evaluation in January, and I took a lot of the exercises from OT and utilized them at home to try and take matters into my own hands while we waited for the January evaluation. It was a refreshing time, but also a very lonely time. At that point, life with Dylan always felt lonely, but it was even lonelier for me without any professional to check in with, other than his pediatrician.

A final word of advice for this chapter: if you think your child might have sensory issues, have himor her evaluated by an OT. I know you're exhausted. I know the idea of having to do one more thing makes you want to hit your head against a wall. Been there, done that, still doing it sometimes! So to help you out, here are the exact steps you should take to make this happen:

- Go to your insurance provider's website.
- Look up OTs in your network by area.
- When you have the list up, start calling those professionals.
- Confirm that they do, in fact, take your insurance. You'd be amazed at how many places say they take your insurance online, only to find out once you get to the appointment that they no longer do. Save yourself the trip and a bad day, and just ask when you call.
- Ask if you need a referral from your pediatrician's office.
- Schedule an appointment.
- Bring all of your child's history with you and a list of questions you want to ask the OT.
- Go to the appointment.

This list also applies to every other health care professional you will end up making an appointment with. These eight steps will make things a lot easier on you and your child.

If you don't have insurance, you should look into other forms of insurance (Medicaid, the Affordable Care Act, or some type of private insurance). Seriously, doctors' bills, therapists, evaluations, and so on are super expensive, and the last thing you want to do is start adding debt to your already stressful life. We had a psychological evaluation done on Dylan, and out of pocket it would have cost us over $600. With our insurance, we paid a co-pay, and that was it.

I'm fortunate that I have a husband who knows the medical system pretty well. He loves to haggle with insurance companies if they give him any problems, and he knows the coding of most appointments. I advise you to find someone like this in your own life. If you are like me and get stressed out at the thought of dealing with money, insurance companies, and so on, ask around. Ask your friends for help understanding the lingo. Put a question out there on Facebook and see if there are any insurance-savvy friends who would be willing to explain things to you. There are also a ton of forums out there with parents going through the exact same thing, so drop in a question, and see if anyone can offer you advice.

I can't tell you how many times we have saved ourselves a co-pay here or there simply because we knew our rights. I can also tell you that we've been in situations where our insurance company has actually sent us a check after the fact. Stay on it, stick with it, and don't let these companies push you around.

Psychological Evaluation

"Why fit in when you were born to stand out?"

– Dr. Seuss

Finally, the day of the test arrived. We met with Dr. Jones for Dylan's psych evaluation, not knowing what to expect. I had called prior to our meeting (which I recommend that all parents do if you are going to have this test done), and I asked as many questions as I could think of. How long is the test? Does Dylan go in alone? Can I bring my other kids? When will I get the results? What do the results mean? Take every single question you have and write it down, and then call the office and ask. Also, call your insurance company PRIOR to the testing to make sure it's covered. This test is super expensive. Like upwards of $600 expensive.

I was sent a packet of information prior to the appointment, which, if you're like me, you'll look forward to filling out. No, seriously. I have always loved to fill out paperwork. Maybe that's the writer side of me? I filled that packet out, making sure every "I" was dotted and every "T" was crossed. I was ready for this appointment.

I was so nervous the day I took Dylan in. Just the thought that I was taking one of my children in for something like this was heartbreaking. I can't tell you how many times I told myself that if I could take these appointments, these exams, these moments from Dylan, I would. I wanted to be the one who experienced the questions and the demands of the medical professionals, because I was better equipped to handle them. I hated that Dylan was the one going through all of these things, and I felt an enormous amount of guilt—so much I can't even begin to describe it, because at times it was too much for me to even comprehend.

I wasn't sure how to tell Dylan about this test, so I just told him we were going back to the therapist's office to see a different doctor who was going to ask him some questions, and that I would be waiting for him in the waiting room. I was told it would take several hours, so I took a seat after I walked Dylan into the office. These moments of waiting are hard. Sometimes I'd see my phone light up with my mom or a friend calling me, but so many times I couldn't and didn't answer it. Sometimes it was all I could do just to keep myself together during these appointments—especially this one. When you have a child, or really any situation in your family that requires so many doctors' appointments, it can be extremely tiring to explain things over and over again. Friends and family mean well when they call to check in, but I have found that it helps to have a point person. That point person is my mom.

My mom is usually the one I tell everything to, and who can calm me down even when I'm hanging off of the highest branch. She's the person who can bring me back to reality and peel away some of the guilt that I carry with me. She tells me I'm a good mom, and I know she means it.

The first part of the process was a clinical interview between

56

me and the pediatric neuropsychologist. This was a meeting for us to go over Dylan's history and what concerns I had. The next part was Dylan undergoing a battery of psychological tests as the handout stated. Dylan's cognitive ability, academic skills, and social/emotional functioning were all tested.

After the testing, I met with the doctor and she explained the results to me. It was a preliminary debriefing of sorts, and I was able to ask questions. A more detailed version of the evaluation was mailed to me one week later.

Dylan was tested for Asperger's, autism, autism spectrum disorder, ADHD, and bipolar, and he showed early signs of bipolar based on what I had shared with the doctor. "Come back when he's seven or eight years old," she told me. "He's too young to be diagnosed with bipolar. Typically, children are not diagnosed with this before six years of age."

She explained to me that at my son's age, kids are still growing and their brains are still developing. To try to diagnose a child at that age would be premature. I was okay with this. While I was sad that he showed signs, I was okay with the results.

There is a history of mental illness on my side of the family, and I had never thought about the possibility of one of my kids inheriting any type of disorder. But when I think about things that have happened right in my own family, I can't help but wonder if it's inevitable that Dylan will one day end up with a mental illness. My aunt Joanne committed suicide ten years ago. My uncle Steven was schizophrenic (he has since passed away), and my uncles Ernie and Larry are both alcoholics. I also have depression, as well as my mom. Mental illness runs rampant in my family, and I guess I shouldn't be surprised that it might rear its ugly head in one of my own.

But bipolar disorder wasn't the only thing Dylan showed signs of. Dylan also scored high for attention deficit hyperactive disorder (ADHD). No surprise here. ADHD also pops up on my side of the family, so one of my offspring was bound to have it. When you're tested for ADHD, you can score as high as forty (the higher the worse). Dylan scored a thirty-six. Okay, while that stunk, I was happy that we at least knew that ADHD was what he had.

We took the results and brought them to Dylan's pediatrician who said that while she could prescribe medication for Dylan's ADHD, she did not feel comfortable doing so because it wasn't her specialty. She referred us on to a pediatric neurologist. This would be our second time seeing a neurologist: the first time when Dylan wasn't walking and now, several years later, for ADHD.

We met with the neurologist, and he looked over Dylan's test results before giving us his own ADHD questionnaire for Dylan's kindergarten teacher to complete. At this time, Dylan was in summer school and hadn't yet started kindergarten. We had his summer school teacher fill out that form to help the neurologist figure out where Dylan was excelling and where he could use some help. It was after this school evaluation that we knew for certain Dylan needed medication.

Dylan was having a hard time sitting still in class, waiting his turn, and not making obnoxious noises while his teacher was talking. I know. This all sounds like a typical five-year-old boy, right? Well, sort of. Take that thought and multiply it by a million, and that's what Dylan looks like.

We started seeing a child therapist who used play therapy as her technique to help children feel more comfortable talking about things. While I'd never taken part in play therapy, I was well versed in the therapist-parent routine during the first session. Dylan stayed in the waiting room and played with toys while I went back to the therapist's office and talked to her about why we were there and what my goals and expectations were.

If I'm being honest, I have to tell you that I went into this next round of therapy with a little less gusto than normal. The therapist reminded me of a young, valley school girl who was preoccupied with other things. I can usually tell within a few minutes of meeting a healthcare professional if I'm going to like them. You might think I have pretty high expectations, but actually, I think I keep the bar at a pretty normal level when it comes to therapists and doctors. I expect that they have a good bedside manner, that they have a good attitude, that they're on time, and that they act in a way in which you can tell that they love their job and are just as committed to helping your family as you are. Let me just say, this is not always the case. The Amy Vaughans are far and few between.

Be prepared to work on your patience, and anticipate that you will have to be the advocate in every situation. I don't tell you this to discourage you, but rather to give you a heads up of sorts when entering into the healthcare world.

Remember, educate yourself on these things. I hear all too often that because things cost so much money, people immediately dismiss the idea of looking into them. I'm here to tell you that yes, up front, it can be scary, but take the time to dissect each appointment, each insurance letter, and each situation that comes your way. The more information you have, the better equipped you will be to make the best decision for your child.

The Medication Train

*"Yesterday is history. Tomorrow is a mystery. Today is a gift.
That's why we call it 'The Present'."*

– Eleanor Roosevelt

Speaking of making the best decisions for your child...let's talk about medication for a minute, because we all know what a tricky subject that can be.

As I said earlier, Dylan's pediatrician agreed to put him on Tenex (guanfacine hydrochloride) in November of 2013 under the supervision of a neurologist, but our first obstacle was that the first neurologist had retired. And the new one? Well, he was just awful.

Dr. T was the only pediatric neurologist in our insurance network, and I had heard from a friend who had taken her daughter to see him that I needed to be prepared because he was extremely difficult to work with. I went into that first appointment with an open mind and walked out in tears.

That first session was for all of us to meet and talk about why Dylan was on medication. Gabe and I went over Dylan's entire history and were about to tell Dr. T about our sixteen-week PCIT course when he said, "Well, I know exactly what the problem is. I see this all the time. You're just bad parents."

The look on my face must have been enough to signal to Gabe that I could not speak. Gabe stepped in and began defending our parenting skills. "If we're such bad parents, why on earth would we have completed a sixteen-week course on how to re-parent our child? We wouldn't be here talking to you if we didn't care about our son."

Dr. T seemed interested in the PCIT course we'd taken and asked us to explain what it was all about. After talking to him about what we'd completed, he changed his tune and complimented us on our efforts. It was still hard for me to accept that a doctor would come right out and say we were bad parents. By all means, if we were, then I would have accepted it, but I knew that Gabe and I had been fighting for our son's happiness since the day he was born.

Dr. T also gave us a questionnaire called, "ADHD Rating Scale-IV" which comes from ADHD Rating Scale-IV: Checklists, Norms, and Clinical Interpretation by George J. DuPaul, Thomas J. Power, Arthur D. Anastopoulos, and Robert Reid. It consists of eighteen questions with four options for each question:

0 = Never or Rarely
1 = Sometimes
2 = Often
3 = Very Often

The idea was to add up the number from each question and the sum of those numbers would be your child's raw score.

Dylan's first score was a thirty. This meant nothing to me at the time, until it was explained to us by Dr. T that a child's range should be between zero and eighteen. And Dylan scored a thirty.

After that first meeting, we had a medication plan set in place for Dylan, and the medication train began. Tenex is often prescribed for ADHD and is an immediate-release drug. This means that it starts working soon after it's taken. We were told to watch for side effects like trouble falling asleep, staying asleep, and loss of appetite.

While Dylan was on medication at school, we gave the questionnaire below to his teacher, and she filled it out every three months. While his number did go down and continued to go down, it was never in the "No ADHD" zone. Because there was no place on this questionnaire to write down specifics, his teacher took it upon herself to send a note home each day from school with details about Dylan's behavior. I was extremely grateful. Not only was I able to be in the know, but I took those notes to his doctor, which gave him a better understanding as to what time of day Dylan would start to fall apart. Those tiny slips of paper with their color coded smiley faces were my lifeline to understanding what Dylan was like when he was not with me, and how we could use his medication to best help him.

10/21/14

8:00 - 9:30	9:30 - 11:00	11:00 - 1:00	1:00 - 3:00
YELLOW	YELLOW	RED	YELLOW
Clipped up for working quietly, then down for jumping and rolling on the carpet, then down again for making silly noises on carpet.	Playing in bathroom.	Continuous noises and rolling around on carpet, asked to sit in hallway for a while, standing up and playing in the hallway.	Clipped up for walking so quietly in the hallway.

The waiting game to see which medications worked and which did not was a trying time. Not just for Gabe and me as parents, but especially for Dylan. I think he's only ever asked us once why he has to take so many pills, to which I replied, "Because it helps you be the best person you can be." How do you even begin to tell your six-year-old child that he has a long list of disorders? My advice—you don't. I did tell him that he had ADHD the day he was diagnosed. I explained to him what it was and how it affected him in his life. I also explained to him that there were lots of people who had ADHD, and it wasn't something that was terrible. "Some of the most creative people have ADHD, Dylan. If we were all the same, that would be boring."

"Like who?" he asked.

"Well, like my brother. Your uncle Donny has ADHD and he lives a great life," I explained.

"You mean the one who was in the war?" he asked.

Laughing, I said, "Yes, the one who was in the war."

"So I can still fight?"

"Huh?" I asked.

"I can still be a soldier?" he asked.

"Yes, you can still be a soldier," I assured him.

Then I got up from the table where we were both sitting and left him to play with his rice bucket. I walked over to the kitchen sink and started loading the dishwasher, wondering if I'd made the right choice to tell him about his diagnosis. While I was thankful for an actual name to what Dylan was going through, I knew that ADHD was not the only disorder he had. I knew there was more to it than just that. I'd grown up with people who had ADHD, and they didn't behave the way Dylan behaved. But I hoped the medication would help.

The decision to put Dylan on medication was extremely painful. I felt like a failure. I still feel like a failure at times. I felt like I was letting him down. I felt like I was letting my husband down and I felt like I was letting myself down. Many times I told myself, "This isn't really as bad as I think it is. Dylan is just a strong-willed child and I can do this. He doesn't need medication." But, we noticed a change in Dylan's behavior after he was prescribed Zoloft for anxiety and depression, Tenex for ADHD, and Risperdal for ODD. I know, that sounds like a lot of medication for such a little boy, and it is.

I often asked myself, how did we get to this point? Why did my child need so many medications just to be able to function like other children his age? To say that I felt that life was unfair and that Dylan had been dealt a bad hand of cards is an understatement, and then add to that my questioning of whether or not we were doing the right thing. I cannot even begin to tell you what it feels like to be the parent who puts their child on medication. But I have always told myself, as hard as it is for me to parent Dylan, it must be a heck of a lot harder to actually be Dylan.

You've probably noticed by now that I talk a lot about guilt in this book, but I don't know how else to help someone understand what this life is like without using the word. By definition it means, "a bad feeling caused by knowing or thinking that you have done something bad or wrong." Notice the word "thinking?" You don't have to actually be guilty of anything to feel that you are. It's a constant struggle, and one that I'm not sure will ever entirely go away. There isn't a day that goes by that I don't feel the enormous weight of my decisions and how they will affect Dylan now and in the future.

Medication:

A SUBSTANCE USED IN TREATING DISEASE OR RELIEVING PAIN*

Medication is one of those tricky subjects we often try to hide. If we're being honest, it can make things a bit awkward. But you have to find other moms who have children who are taking meds for ADHD, and then you'll know that you are part of a much larger, often silent group of people who really do know what you're going through. I met one such mom in MOPS. In one of my prayer requests, I asked for prayer for Dylan and for his med situation.

"My son's on that too," she said.

"Really?" I asked. "How are you getting through this?"

And with that, our conversation began around our two boys who were both on medication for ADHD. It helped. Even though her son was quite a bit older and our situations were quite a bit different, the feelings of sadness were still there for us to share. For the first time, I felt comfort in knowing that I could talk to someone about what I was going through. And that helped, especially when Gabe and I didn't know how to approach the school setting with a child on medication.

Do we tell his teacher? Do we not say anything? The school somewhat knew that he was taking medication because I had

Source: Merriam-Webster's Learner's Dictionary

to fill out his medical paperwork at open house. I remember sitting in the elementary school at one of the lunch tables they had set up, across from a friend of mine. At that time, I hadn't told anyone that Dylan had started meds, so I was sitting there kind of looking into thin air, thinking, How do I answer these questions? It was like they were asking me to sum up all of my child's history in two sentences, when I'd had five years of this craziness. How do I tell them that yes, my child has behavioral issues, and yes, he has trouble following rules, but he is still a good boy and yes, he is taking meds and this is what they are.

The school nurse happened to walk by, and I made rookie mistake number one. This is what *not* to do when you're enrolling your child into school for the first time.

"Hi, um, are you the school nurse?" I asked.

"Yessssss," she drew out.

"So, my son will be starting kindergarten, and I'm having trouble filling this part out." (I point to the part where it asks if your child is on medication, and if yes, for what and how much).

"Well, is your son taking medication?" she asked.

"Well, yes." I said. "But I don't want to put it on here because I don't want people to judge him."

"Umm, well, ma'am, you have to write it down," she protested. "No one is going to judge him."

I wanted to believe her so badly, but I was afraid to put the "real" stuff down on paper. I felt like I had made a huge mistake by even asking her what to do, because it made me look unsure about my own son. It made me sound embarrassed and insecure. Worst of all, it made me cry, and it brought me face-to-face with another adult who would only know my son by the names of his medications instead of the little boy beneath the disorders. My mama heart just fell to pieces at that moment. I knew that this school thing was going to be hard for Dylan and hard for me. I looked down the halls to my right and to my left. I thought back to my childhood in elementary school and knew that Dylan was going to have a hard road ahead of him. Not because I had a hard time in elementary school, but just because kids can be mean, and especially to kids that are different.

It was the end of July, and already it felt like I was about to embark on yet another stage of life with Dylan. My emotions were all over the place: I was excited about him starting school and excited about him getting older, but obviously sad because who wants to wish away their child's adolescence? It's not supposed to be that way. That became even clearer when we had Hannah and then another daughter, Elinor.

As Gabe and I watched the two of them grow up, interact, and become sweet little girls, it became crystal clear that Dylan really wasn't acting the way a normal little boy was supposed to act. Things that kids enjoyed doing, he didn't. Methods of discipline that worked for most kids didn't work on Dylan. I also worried a lot about his sisters seeing Dylan's behavior and thinking it was okay to act like that. I had so much guilt surrounding this area of my parenting that I could spend countless nights just worrying about it alone, but that's where my faith came in.

I didn't start going to church until I was seven months pregnant with Dylan. Gabe and I had tried to have a baby for nearly two years, and, after several doctors' appointments for both of us, we were told it would be very difficult for us to have children. When we finally got pregnant, I still felt like something was missing. Actually, I had felt a void my whole life and I knew I needed something. Something bigger than me, bigger than Gabe, and bigger than anyone I knew. When I was little, even though I wasn't raised in any sort of religion, I used to talk to someone "up there," and that feeling never left me. I took all of those old feelings and my new feelings as a soon-to-be mom and walked into the Methodist church where we lived. I didn't know anyone there, but I knew I needed to hear something.

When I walked inside and sat down, I just teared up. Today, I don't remember what the message was about, but that day it was what I needed. I continued to go every Sunday and started to meet people along the way. Gabe didn't come with me until he was ready, but he eventually joined me once Dylan was born. Since Dylan was so difficult as a newborn, I prayed a lot. I didn't really know how to pray or what that looked like, but I talked to God and begged Him to fix Dylan. I begged Him to show me what was wrong with this baby and how to help him.

As the years went on, we continued to go to church, eventually switching from the Methodist to the Christian church across the street. The days got harder with Dylan, but my faith got stronger. I hear people say that when life is hard and it feels like you have to fall to your knees each day, that is where God meets you to lift you up. I do believe this, and although I sometimes feel alone in this journey with Dylan, I do feel that He is helping me. One of my favorite verses that I repeat over and over again is from Matthew 11:28 (NIV): "Come to me, all you who are weary and burdened, and I will give you rest." It hits home with me because I'm weary. I'm burdened. I'm desperate for rest. But God is always there.

Kindergarten

"Wherever you go, go with all your heart."
– Confucius

As I said in the last chapter, in this time of entering kindergarten, I was definitely worried about how Dylan would behave in school. Yes, he went to preschool, but this was different. This would be all day, and I would not be texting with his teacher throughout the day like I was able to do with his preschool teacher. I was nervous for Dylan, for my family, and for his teacher.

While we included Dylan's medical information on his enrollment papers, we did not make it a point to tell his teacher about all of the struggles we had been having. We decided to let things go as they may and deal with them as they came. And I think we made the right choice.

As far as I know, there is no parent manual on how to prepare your behaviorally-inept child from entering the mainstream world. There is no book on what to do when your child comes home in tears because he is so tired from holding it all together at school that he just falls apart at home. And there is certainly no resource out there that tells you not to sign your kid up for T-ball when that's what every other kid in his class is doing. We found out the hard way that group sports just wasn't something Dylan was ready for. Looking back, maybe Gabe knew that all along, especially considering that I had to convince my husband that T-ball would be "fun."

"This is what kids do, honey," I explained. "Dylan needs to do normal things with other kids. Maybe the exercise will be good for him?"

There were a few moments during Dylan's stint with T-ball that actually made me feel like a normal mom with a normal boy. I remember inviting my in-laws to one of his games and laying a blanket out on the field. The girls and I sat on the blanket, and Mom, Dad, and Gabe sat in the lawn chairs. We hooted and hollered for Dylan as he went up to bat for the first time. Inside, I was a ball of emotions. *Wow. This is awesome. My little boy is growing up. Okay, this is going to be okay. Things feel normal.*

That was the start of the season. We ended the season with Gabe running out onto the field, hoisting Dylan over his shoulders while Dylan was screaming and kicking, and making a beeline to the car. You see, Dylan had a problem with paying attention on the field, and he would completely ignore his coaches when they told him to stop teasing the other players. If Dylan went for a ball and another kid did too, well, that was grounds for a tantrum. If Dylan was up to bat and missed the ball, well, here comes the crazy face. If Dylan's friend was playing second base with him and they were supposed to be taking turns going for the ball, well, Dylan would make sure he went for it every single time. So T-ball was OUT, if you'll excuse the pun.

During this time, life at home wasn't getting any easier, and life at school seemed to be getting harder. I found out Dylan had been separated from his peers at lunch and made to sit at a desk by himself in the cafeteria. No one at the school told me this was happening. I only found out because Dylan decided to tell me on one of the many tearful rides home from picking him up after school. How did I not know about this? I wondered, tears crowding my own eyes at the look on his face. Maybe because I hoped silence meant everything was going okay, and I know now that it just isn't safe to assume that. I'm telling you this because you have to be an advocate for your child. As much as you want to give them space to let them grow, you still have to make sure that their best interest is at play while they're not in your presence.

I got in touch with Dylan's teacher and asked her about the separation at lunch. "Yes," she said. "They moved him to his own desk because he was disrupting the other kids from eating."

While I was obviously upset about this and my mama heart broke for him as I pictured him eating his lunch all alone, I also understood. I understood that it wasn't fair to the other kids who could sit still and eat their lunch. It wasn't fair to the parents who trusted that their children were getting the time they needed to eat their lunch without being continually interrupted, bothered, or annoyed. But it still hurt.

We were able to work through the lunchroom situation with his teacher, and with a few consecutive days of good behavior in the cafeteria, Dylan was allowed to sit back at the table with his classmates. The classroom was a different story. It wasn't until the school year was over that I heard about how much Dylan was put in the hallway for disrupting the class. I found this out from one of our neighbors the day we were moving out of our home in Missouri. She was pulling out of her driveway and she called me over. "I don't know how to tell you this," she said, "but your son was unfairly treated at school."

I started to get upset. "What do you mean?" I asked.

"Well, I sub there a lot, you know. And sometimes I subbed right across the hallway from his classroom. He spent more time out in that hallway than he did in the actual class. I've never seen a kid spend that much time in the hallway, and I've been teaching for a long time. They didn't treat him right."

My heart was beating nearly out of my chest at this point. Images of Dylan alone in the hallway flooded my head, and I started to panic. "Who didn't treat him right?" I asked.

"His teacher. All of them. No one treated him right."

I never found out what happened. School was out for the summer, and I had no clue where to begin. I thought about calling the school district, but how would I approach the subject? I asked Dylan about it, and he agreed that he was in the hallway a lot, but I'm not sure that he had anything to compare it to. It was his first year of school, and with his low self-esteem, I'm guessing he assumed that he deserved to be in the hallway, which is why he never told me.

While I was obviously upset and confused, it was hard for me to process this information because I had made sure to have great communication with his teacher throughout the entire year. I would have gone so far as to say that she was a key component, and really, a catalyst for making sure that Dylan succeeded as much as possible while at school.

She made special progress charts tailored just to Dylan's behavior and sent them home in his folder. She used a color system (pink meant you had a great day, purple was good, green was where each student started their day—kind of the neutral spot, ready to learn—yellow was making a bad choice, orange was a warning, and red was a letter home to your parents). This helped me gauge where Dylan was at each day, but for Dylan, the colors would become something he got really angry and hurt about.

For example, if you stayed on pink all day, you got to pick a treasure out of the toy box. After days of trying to "be good," Dylan just couldn't quite get to pink. This resulted in him being extremely difficult when he got into the car from the pickup line. He would throw his backpack inside the van, stomp back to his seat, and refuse to put his seatbelt on. The once calm atmosphere I had in the car with the girls was once again ruined by the presence of his never-ending tantrums. I dreaded picking him up from school.

Thankfully, his teacher thought it would be a good idea to alter Dylan's reward chart. If she knew Dylan was really trying to behave that day, she would let him pick a toy. Small efforts like this made a huge impact on Dylan's self-esteem. So how did we go from there to spending all day in the hallway?

We also had his teacher fill out the ADHD questionnaire given to us by the neurologist every few months. This helped determine if the meds were working and how long they were working.

When we realized that Dylan was doing well in the mornings at school, but getting really hyper after lunch, we brought that information to his neurologist who thought maybe Dylan needed to start taking a longer-acting drug, something like Concerta. At this time, Dylan was taking Focalin for ADHD, Risperdal for ODD, and Zoloft for anxiety. We took him off the Focalin and put him on

Concerta. Again, I found nothing in my library of books that told me or prepared me for what med changes were like with a child, and I desperately needed someone to prepare me for what was going to happen. If you're going through this, please know there are a few things you can do to make it easier on both you and your child. I figured these things out by trial and error, but I hope they help you avoid some of the difficulty we faced.

- **If there is a weaning protocol from moving from one drug to another, follow it to a "T."** That means, if you must slowly take your child off of one drug to introduce another drug, do it exactly as your doctor has explained. If you sometimes get confused or don't really understand how to do that (like me), ask your pharmacist. Doctors don't always do the best at explaining what their directions mean in a real-life-at-home type of setting.

- **Be aware of the side effects of each drug.** Research them on your own (because your doctor won't always tell you all of the side effects) and write your questions down. For example, the Risperdal we put Dylan on has a side effect of weight gain, so much so that I have learned this drug is very controversial when given to children. I've read one too many testimonials from parents who say their child took this drug and gained fifty pounds, but when they took them off of it, they still couldn't get the weight off. I've read about the lack of sleep, loss of appetite, dry mouth, upset stomach, and on and on and on. All of this to say, try and read up on as much as you can about the drug.

- **Watch your child closely for signs that something isn't right.** For a short two days, Dylan was switched to Adderall, and it was the worst thing ever. I noticed that he was a completely different child, down to the smallest detail. His eyes were completely glossed over, he was very fidgety, and overall he was very detached from our family. I knew right away that this wasn't the right medication for him. However, that's not to say it isn't the right med for your child because they affect each one differently. But I knew we needed to get him off of that one right away.

- **Most of these drugs cost a lot of money.** I'm talking in the hundreds of dollars. Thankfully, our co-pays are usually ten dollars or less. Usually. There was one medication that Dylan was taking that, even with our co-pay, was going to be around forty-five dollars per pill. Gabe happens to work with some pharmacists in his line of work and mentioned the cost of the pill to one of them. This person then told him that her son was on the same thing and that there was a manufacturer's coupon that would allow us to get it for free. Yes. Yes. Yes. FREE. Google the maker of the drug and see if they have a coupon for you to download and print. Take that to your pharmacist. Ask your pharmacist if you need to print it out every time you get a refill or if they can keep it on file. Yes, it's that easy. Why doctors don't tell you this, I have no idea.

- **Be patient.** While this is new for you, it's also new and frightening for your child. I had to remember that Dylan's body was getting used to coming off of one med only to be introduced to another right away. He's six. He doesn't know what's going on, and I can't expect him to. I had to remind myself that it takes time to see results, and I must be patient with the process.

- **Stay vigilant** and watch for ANY behavioral changes.

During one of our med changes, towards the end of the school year, Dylan's neurologist bumped up his dosage of Zoloft and put him on Adderall. Dylan and Hannah had gotten into a fight in the garage over a balloon. He pushed her, she started crying, and I sent him up to his room. A few minutes later he came outside, ran down our driveway, and into the road.

"Dylan, what are you doing?" I screamed. "Get out of the road!"

"I want to die," he yelled. "I want to be with Jesus! I hate you! I hate living here!"

"Bubby, get out of the road," Hannah pleaded. Crying, she ran to him.

"Dylan and Hannah, get out of the road!" I screamed again.

Dylan never came back to the house on his own. I had to run out into the road and get down on my knees with him.

"Dylan, why are you saying that?" I asked. "Why are you saying you don't want to live?"

"Because I hate it here," he cried. "You're not fair. You don't listen to me. I just want to be with Jesus. I don't want to be here on earth."

I took Dylan by the hand, scooped Hannah up with my other arm, and walked towards the garage where Elinor was screaming for me. I took all three kids back into the house and cried for as long as I could remember. I called Gabe and told him what was going on. He came home from work, we talked to Dylan together, and then we tried to go on with the rest of our day as normal. I remember this day being really hard on all of us. Unfortunately, this wouldn't be the last time Dylan would talk about dying.

Possibly one of the worst things about this whole thing was the response I got from the neurologist's office when I called to seek advice about what to do. Again, there is no handbook labeled "What to Do When Your Child Says He Wants to Die." I called the office, asked to speak to a nurse, and told her what happened. She didn't seem alarmed in the least bit, told me Dr. T was on vacation, and that was that. To me, this was not okay. So I called their office back and asked to talk with the nurse again. It seemed that Dr. T's nurse was on vacation too, and actually, so was most of the staff. The nurse I did talk to was not able to tell me what I should do.

"Well, what do you do when a child does this? How do I handle this? What do I say to him? Do I stop his meds? Do I decrease them? Do I keep him home from school tomorrow? Do I tell his teacher what happened to give her a heads up? He has a field trip tomorrow. Is it safe for him to go? He won't be in the same town as me if something happens and I need to get to him. Is it okay to let him out of my sight?"

I got nothing but silence on the other end of the line.

"Dr. T says if you feel like he is that much of a threat, you should admit him to the hospital," the nurse said.

"Really?" I asked in disbelief. "Don't you think taking him to the hospital and having him admitted will scare him? He's acting fine right now, and I'm afraid if I do that, he will be so scared."

"Yeah. I don't know," she said.

Okay, so I don't know much about office protocol, but I'm pretty sure that this was not the right answer for her to give me. Maybe the most politically correct answer to make sure they weren't sued for telling me not to go to the hospital, but not the best answer. Certainly not the answer I was looking for, which would have been something like, "Let me have Dr. T call you," or "We have a doctor filling in for Dr. T while he's on vacation. Let me have him call you in a few minutes," or "Yes, we have a protocol for this if a child threatens suicide, and this is what it is."

This was one of many times when I felt like a health care professional had let me down. I talked with Gabe about it and shared the situation with my mom, and both told me to let Dylan go on the field trip since he was acting his normal self again. That next day was awful for me. I worried about Dylan the entire time. While I didn't tell his teacher the details of what had happened, I did tell her that Dylan had had an extremely difficult day after school, and if she could keep an extra eye on him during the field trip, I would appreciate it. Not only did she say yes, but she texted me a picture of Dylan on the bus with a huge smile on his face. That teacher knew what this mama needed, and it was reassurance.

We got through that day and moved on to the next and the next. Since that terrible day, we have moved from Missouri to Arkansas because of Gabe's job, and while I love it here, things have taken a turn for the worse with Dylan. This is my first summer with Dylan home, without meds, and with two other children to parent. After being approached by our pharmacist who was concerned about the amount of medication Dylan was taking, we talked to him about the possibility of weaning him off of everything.

"It's worth a try," he said.

Now I do understand that pharmacists are not necessarily pediatricians or neurologists, and this is something that I should have run by Dylan's doctors. However, this pharmacist seemed to know what he was talking about and I trusted him. We lived in a small town, and he was familiar with what Dylan had been prescribed, taken off of, and then prescribed again. I couldn't help but agree with him that I would like to know what Dylan was like without meds. I started to wonder if I was making all of this bad behavior up in my head and, if I'd only take Dylan off of his meds, I'd see that he was just fine—that he actually didn't need to be on any medication at all.

I followed the pharmacist's instructions about weaning so that we were doing it safely, but it was clear, very soon, that Dylan could not function without meds. Our days became very much what they used to be—filled with endless amounts of crying, yelling, screaming, defiance, and anger. It broke my heart to see him struggling. Gabe and I talked and decided to slowly put him back on all of his meds. It was hard for me to accept the reality of what was. A part of me had always hoped that we were all wrong about Dylan and that what he really needed was to just be his organic, raw self. I have a hard time with this every day.

To say that I am counting down the days until school starts would be an understatement, and that's one of the crappy things about all of this. I've done nothing but wish away the years with Dylan, when what I really want is to slow down and enjoy each minute I have before he's grown. It doesn't work that way with kids who have behavioral issues, though. It's like I've been robbed of his childhood and so has he.

Dylan at Wild Kratts during his Kindergarten year.

I try to stay on top of these feelings because they have a tendency to pull me down and away from what really matters, which is being the best parent I can be for Dylan. However, there is still that sense of loss when I think about not being able to do and enjoy the milestones of his childhood like I have with his sisters. Watching him take his first steps was amazing, but it took two years to get there. Listening to him fall asleep and sleep through the entire night for the first time at fifteen months was comforting, but it took over a year of sleepless nights to get there. Being able to go out to dinner as a family is something we still long to do. So far it's been six, almost seven years since we could.

When I hear about my friends going out for pizza or taking their kids on vacation, I can't help but feel a pang of jealousy. I want that so badly for my family. On the rare occasion that Dylan is somewhere else for the day, the four of us can function as a unit, and we are able to go out and about without worrying what might happen. I love that, but I hate knowing the reality of our situation, which is that we cannot take Dylan out in public. Sure, he has moments of being okay, but for the most part, he is too much of a liability, and he flat out stresses me out.

I recently went to a chocolate factory where the kids and I made candy. This is something I've been doing for several years now, but Dylan has usually been at school. Since this year's activity was during the summer, he was with me when I drove the hour away to get to the factory, meeting a friend and her four girls there. I think I had so much anxiety about how Dylan was going to behave that I didn't get to enjoy the actual candy-making process. He would be okay for one second, and then he'd get out of his seat, make weird awkward noises the next, and look at me with those crazy eyes, trying to get me mad. It was awful. It took all the fun out of watching Hannah make her chocolate sunshine cookie and put all the attention on making sure that Dylan didn't ruin some other kid's masterpiece.

That's the thing with this. There's no rhyme or reason to what happens next. Dylan can be quiet and well-behaved one minute and then rude, crass, and disrespectful the next. Today, we're in the middle of a heat wave, and it's too hot for the kids to play outside, which means I'm stuck inside with Dylan all day. I don't think anyone knows how terrifying that is except for another parent who has a child with ODD, ADHD, and any other behavioral disorder.

It. Is. Debilitating.

Thankfully, I have found ways to keep myself grounded and sane. Since we've moved, this is probably the best I've ever taken care of myself. I'm eating healthy, I'm still in Weight Watchers, and I work out almost every day (whether I want to or not). And really, the time away from the kids, combined with the exertion that comes from being physical, feels so good after a stressful day. It keeps me from flying off the handle and keeps me in check. I've also started doing yoga again, which I haven't done since before I had kids. It's something I've always enjoyed but just never had access to or made time for. My first time back at yoga was just over a month ago, and the tears just started rolling down my face as I sat there and listened to the teacher tell us to get into a meditative state. It was hard to quiet my head, but it was so peaceful once I did. It was like I could finally breathe again in that moment that was just for me.

Sometimes I dread waking up in the morning because I know I have to somehow figure out how to get through another day with Dylan's disorders. I have to somehow figure out a way to enjoy my time with the girls without them losing their innocence from the vulgar things Dylan shouts within the walls of our home. I have to make myself not think of what they must be thinking about their big brother and how that's shaping their little brains, because if I do, if I really stop and worry about what they might remember from their childhood, I'll let his illness consume me. And while I love Dylan beyond words and grieve that he has to deal with these issues, I'm a parent to more than one child. My responsibility is not just to him. I must also protect his sisters and myself as well.

Siblings

"Siblings are the people we practice on, the people who teach us about fairness and cooperation and kindness and caring - quite often the hard way."
– Pamela Dugdale

We were getting ready to celebrate Dylan's second birthday the morning I found out I was pregnant. Gabe and I were told that we might never have kids and here we were, pregnant with our second and so excited (but nervous) about starting the journey again. We had said, at one point after having Dylan, that we would not try for any more kids since he was so difficult. Raising him had taken the fun out of our lives and our marriage, and we weren't sure we wanted to do it again. But, as with any pregnancy news, there's no helping getting excited.

My pregnancy was harder the second time around because I threw up a lot more. I knew fairly early on that it was probably a girl because this pregnancy was so different from my first one. I was sick almost every morning of the first and second trimester. All of the tricks I had read about—saltines, ginger ale, the BRAT diet (bananas, rice, applesauce and toast)—did not work. None of those things ever sounded good to me. I ended up taking medication to help with the nausea.

Things got worse at home. Dylan was two and a half, and I was about seven months pregnant. His tantrums lasted hours. Literally, hours. When I would try and calm him down or put him in time out, whatever the situation, he would bite, kick, hit, and spit at me. Not that this was okay by any means, but the fact that I was pregnant made it a lot harder for me deal with.

When Hannah was born, Gabe and I saw more clearly what we already knew: Dylan was different. Hannah was hitting all of her milestones just like babies do. She slept through the night soon after we had her and only fussed when she was hungry or wet. What would my life have been like if I had had her first? I thought.

I used to take the kids to the mall play area for something to do. I'd watch Hannah bravely jump off the foam animals that were mounted to the play mat floor while Dylan watched. I could tell that he wanted to do the same but was scared. It was something we had worked on in physical therapy. Martha would meet me at a park sometimes, and we would practice with Dylan going down the slide or taking steps up the stairs to reach the top of the play set. It was now time for him to take what he'd learned and use it in the play area at the mall.

I struggled with watching Hannah do so many things before Dylan. I felt like their roles were reversed. He was supposed to be the big brother who showed her how to take risks and lead the way, but it was the other way around. I tried hard to stay on equal ground with both kids. If Hannah did something cool, I told her. If Dylan did something cool, I told him. I tried to treat them both the same.

This was not always easy. Hannah showed me that she loved me in so many ways. She said it, she hugged me, kissed me, and generally wanted to please me by doing what she was told. Dylan, on the other hand, would not let me hold him, hug him, or get near him. For the longest time, it felt like he hated me. He favored his dad most of the time—well, all the time, really—and I took that hard. I questioned my ability to mother him. Was I doing something wrong? Did I damage him in some way? Was I too much of a helicopter mom? Had I not let him become who he needed to be?

But Hannah has only ever known her brother to be just the way he is. From the moment we brought her home from the hospital, she has always had a front row seat to his theatrics. Good, bad, or indifferent, Hannah has always had his back. One of the first questions we were always asked at our various doctors' appointments with Dylan was what his relationship was like with Hannah, and did he ever show signs of wanting to hurt her? Our answers were always the same. They had a great relationship and no, he never showed signs of wanting to hurt her, even now, as the two of them are getting older. Sure, they have their typical sibling fights here and there, but for the most part, Dylan includes her, shares with her, and protects her just like a big brother should.

Hannah never said anything during her brother's tantrums. Sometimes I would tell her to leave the room, or I would put Dylan in time-out, and she and I would leave the room. There were plenty of times when we'd have plans to do things as a family only to have to cancel at the last minute because of how Dylan was acting. It was almost impossible to take Dylan out in public because he was that out of control, but Gabe and I didn't feel like that was fair to Hannah, so we did our best to take them out when we felt like we had enough patience to handle him. Even though Dylan is able to function for most of the day, I can tell immediately what kind of day he is going to have. I know when it's not worth it to take him out. I know when it's asking too much of him to pull his stuff together and keep himself in check for just a little bit longer. Gabe and I know when one of us needs to stay home while the other runs a quick errand because Dylan is having a bad day.

Dylan, Hannah and Elinor looking comfy on a long car ride home

Sometimes other family members would say to me, "I just wonder what Hannah thinks?" or "I wonder how this is affecting Hannah?" or "Have you thought about putting Hannah in therapy?" I know these were all well-intentioned questions, but they just added to my already guilt-burdened heart. Did people really think that I hadn't thought about those things? Of course I worried about how this would negatively affect Hannah. But if I allowed those thoughts to take over my energy, what good would that do? So I did the only think I knew how to do and that was love her.

I loved on her as much as she would let me, and the same for Elinor when she came around. I will say, Gabe and I just have to laugh it off when Dylan is screaming in the car and his two sisters are looking at him like, *what planet are you from?* Hannah has learned to ignore it, and Elinor just stares at Dylan and then looks at me and then back at Dylan. If anyone should be screaming in the car, you'd think it'd be the baby in our family and not the six-year-old.

We went to a local fair the other day, and this very thing happened. We were pulling out of our garage on a Saturday afternoon, and I was feeling happy that our little family was taking time out of our laissez-faire weekend to enjoy some fried dough and bounce houses with each other. Gabe hadn't even put the car in drive after backing up when Dylan started screaming, hollering, and making a fuss over his seatbelt.

"It doesn't feel right!" he screamed. "Ahhh! I hate this stupid car!"

And there went my vision for the perfect day. Then I let the situation and my vision of how the day should have gone stress me out and engaged in an ongoing screaming match with him.

"Dylan, pull yourself together and put your seatbelt on. It's not that big of a deal!" I screamed. Yeah. That wasn't helpful.

Why I still do this, I have no idea. I think it's my most common reaction when he starts acting out. I usually have three modes: 1) I ignore him; 2) I am patient and try to help him work out whatever he is dealing with; or 3) Yell back. I was obviously at mode three this day.

Gabe suggested we just stay home, but I refused. "No way," I said. "I'm not going to let him ruin this for the girls. I've already told them we'd take them to the fair."

I looked back in the car at my three children, and my heart hurt for my girls, but my heart also hurt for Dylan. I don't think he would have chosen this life for himself. Who likes to get yelled at by their parents? Who likes to be the one blamed for his sisters not being able to go places? My mama heart hurt for lashing out at him. The verse, "I can do all things through Christ who strengthens me," kept replaying in my mind. I took a deep breath and reached for Gabe's hand.

I will say it's gotten easier as he's gotten older. Everyone told me this. By everyone, I mean the online communities I subscribe to and the books I've read. It does get easier, but there's a huge feeling of sadness that comes from that. Who wants to wish away their son's childhood? It's definitely not something I'd ever imagined I'd be doing. After watching Hannah and Elinor in their baby years, I mourn the loss of never having that precious experience with Dylan.

It's too difficult for me to even look at Dylan's baby pictures or go through his baby book with him. There are too many sad faces and terrible memories to go with each and every one of them. I know I'm a good mom. I do. But there is this huge feeling of insecurity surrounding my parenting of Dylan. Sometimes I feel like I failed him. Why wasn't I more patient? Why wasn't I more understanding? Why did I think it was okay to spank him as much as I did? Why did I think it was okay to utter the words "weird" and "crazy" in his presence? Why did I choose to believe his friends' words over his? These questions haunt me every day, but I have to let some of this guilt go, and the first step is admitting where I went wrong. If I put it out there for you to see, maybe I can help you not make my mistakes.

But if mistakes are good for one thing, it's learning along the way. And I have. I've learned how to be a mom to three kids all at the same time. I've learned how to set Dylan up for success in certain situations like group play. By group play, I mean more than one person playing. So when Dylan and his sisters are playing, I make sure that Dylan has what he needs (rice bucket, sensory Play-Doh, gum to chew, and so on), while I get his sisters set up with some coloring books and crayons. He can still parallel play (play side-by-side with another child), but it helps if he is focused on something that will keep his attention. If I tend to the girls first and leave Dylan last, he will get into trouble, mischief—you name it. I know now that the girls are capable of waiting. They have patience and they have come to accept Dylan. I heard once that, if you ever want to know how to treat your child with special needs, watch how his siblings treat him. That is so true. My girls love on Dylan like he is the cream of the crop. They know no different. They ask about him when he's at school and wake up from naps wanting to play with him. There are no grudges held by them, and there are no pent up words of harshness for him to hear. There's only love, just like it should be.

There are things I would do differently if I'd been given the chance to do them over. I would have asked for help more often. I would have built a support system sooner and surrounded myself with close-knit friends who believed in me and encouraged me to let my child be whoever he needed to be. But this book is not just about helping you see where I went wrong. This book is also about giving you the confidence to say that you did the best you could. And you know what? That's enough.

There were too many times when I would get odd stares and nasty whispers about how my child was acting, and I would feel judgment and shame. I know it's easy for people looking in to say, "Wow, that kid is out of control." I'll admit it, I did it to people all the time before I had kids of my own. Let's just say I have a much different view of things now that I'm sitting in the driver's seat, and I try to extend as much grace as I possibly can to those parents I see with children who might not be acting in such a way that is acceptable to others.

We aren't ever going to be perfect. Every parent makes mistakes, even ones with typical children. But our children aren't typical, and we need to give ourselves some slack and lend grace to one another and to ourselves whenever we can. This includes your spouse as well.

Havoc on My Marriage

"This too shall pass."

– My mother

I read somewhere that married couples who have a child in the home with ODD have a 95 percent divorce rate. I shared that with Gabe and, while we both had a "wow" look on our faces, we completely believed it. Our marriage has been very difficult. I think being married is hard enough with the ups and downs of watching each other grow and become different people, but when you add a child like Dylan into the mix, things get a lot more complicated. Communication breaks down because you're so tired from dealing with your child all day that the last thing you want to do is try and explain something to your spouse. Sex is also something that gets put on the back burner because really, who wants to be touched at the end of the night when you've already been someone's human punching bag?

This feeling hit its boiling point and nearly destroyed my marriage. It was summer, and I was outside playing with Dylan and Hannah in our driveway. I was pregnant with Ellie still, but just a few months away from having her. It was the weekend, and I had wanted all of us to go strawberry picking that morning. Gabe had other plans. He wanted to go golfing with his dad. Now, you must know, this golfing thing was kind of a thorn in my side. Not because I didn't want to encourage Gabe to do the things that made him happy, but because I felt like he did things all the time for himself and I didn't. He was still taking his annual trip to Las Vegas with his college buddies to watch March Madness. He was still driving to Ohio to go golfing with his buddies for a weekend. And he was playing golf with his dad that one Saturday morning. To put it bluntly, I was mad.

Just once, I wanted him to not go anywhere. I had built-up emotions of him leaving for Vegas every year, regardless of whether or not we'd just had a baby. I was angry that he could leave and I couldn't. I was angry that he felt no guilt for leaving us when I wouldn't have, had I ever been given the opportunity. I was angry that he went to work every day and had a normal life from eight to five, while I was trying not to get bitten, spit on, and kicked. I was angry that he wanted to go golfing with his dad on the weekend when all I wanted to do was go strawberry picking and feel like a normal family.

I ended up taking Dylan and left Hannah with Gabe. I peeled out of the driveway with the idea that I would be coming back in time for him to leave with his dad. I got lost on the way there and on the way home. I was late getting back, which meant Gabe was going to be late meeting his dad. I could tell he was mad. I could see he was over it. We started screaming at each other in the driveway, and I begged him not to leave for golf, but there was no convincing him. I just wanted him to hold me and tell me he loved me, but then he started walking towards his car and I started bawling. Like fall to the floor, hyperventilating crying. I texted him through my tears and told him I wanted a divorce.

I called my mom and told her what I'd just done. Divorce was something that had run through my mind very often, actually. I'd thought about it a lot and wondered if my life would be easier without Gabe in it. I played out how things would be in my head…we would share custody of the kids, he would be able to do whatever he wanted to do, and same with me. I would no longer feel so much anger towards him, and, best of all, we wouldn't be fighting in front of the kids anymore.

During those earlier years, we'd lost who we were in the process of raising kids. We had forgotten about all of the funny quirks we'd once loved about each other and replaced them with bitter words about whose parenting style was better. The thought of our dating days in college was too hard for me to ponder, so I just pushed them out of my mind and focused on the task at hand—saving my marriage.

When you're looking for help, you tend to go into survival mode. Well, at least I did. I was basically just surviving this season of our lives, our marriage, and my role as a mom. I was waiting for the storm to pass and for things to get better. When communicating with your own partner becomes part of the problem, it can start to feel like you are drowning with no safety net in sight.

Talking with Theresa and my mom through this time was hard, but necessary. Theresa held me accountable, while my mom gave me the hope to see it through. They each provided me with what I needed to put one foot in front of the other and stay focused on what was important: saving my marriage because it was and is worth it.

Gabe and I still have our moments, but what marriage doesn't? I love that we can tell when the other person has had too much, and our patience is short with Dylan. I love that we can and will jump in for one another when we see the other struggling. It's taken years for us to be at this point, but things are good, and we are better parents because of it. Please know that my heart hurts for you if this is where you're at, but I'm praying for you. And as my mom has told me so many times, "This too shall pass." If your marriage is struggling, here are some things that helped my husband and me reconnect, and I hope they can work for you as well:

- **Go on dates.** Everyone told me this, but it was nearly impossible without family nearby, and I didn't trust anyone enough to stay with Dylan. We were worried that there wasn't a babysitter who existed that could handle Dylan's tantrums. If this is where you're at, plan a date at home. Seriously. When you put your kids to bed, get some wine, beer, or whatever you like to drink, and play cards. Get a board game or work on a puzzle together. Gabe and I still do this since we don't like to spend an arm and a leg on paying a babysitter. Our go-to is Scrabble or watching a movie on Netflix while scarfing down Sonic blizzards.

- **Write loves notes.** Who doesn't love a good ol' love note? I know I do. I make Gabe's lunch every day, so I usually try and stick a little note into his bag that tells him I love him. Send your spouse a text just to let him know you're thinking about him. Gabe doesn't always reciprocate with love notes because that's not his love language, but he does do things like schedule me a facial or send me to the spa because he knows that makes me feel loved and taken care of.

- **Communicate honestly and often**. What does this even mean? Well, it means that you need to check in with one another every day. Yes, every day. Don't hold things in until they come bursting out of you. Talk about the hard things, the fun, and the not-so-fun things. It will clear your mind of clutter, and it will hold the both of you accountable for your feelings.

- **Respect.** It goes a long way. Showing your spouse that you respect him is like telling him you appreciate what he does every day. This isn't my strongest suit. I don't always tell Gabe that I respect and appreciate him, so this is an area I am currently working on. But I do know that when I do tell him, I can see his whole demeanor change. It's like he feels validated in some way, that what he does matters. When I see him happy, it makes me happy.

- **Have a sense of humor.** When our days are long with the kids, we try to have a good laugh about it. There have been a few times when Dylan has done something odd and really, all we can do is make a joke of it to ourselves, because if we don't, this whole journey will consume us. I'm not saying make fun of your child. I'm saying to find humor in the painful moments.

- **Have each other's backs.** This is a big one for me. I have always felt like Gabe has had my back. I can't say it's been the other way around. No matter what my feelings may be towards Dylan and the way he behaves, Gabe has never made me feel guilty for them. This is probably one of the things I love most about him. I'm imperfect, and he loves me in his own perfect way.

I encourage you to think about the things that first attracted you to your partner. Are those things you still love? Or do those things annoy you now? Do you see yourself with this person in the future? Does that make you excited? Ask yourself some hard, real-life questions before you call it quits. Marriage is worth saving if it's a healthy situation.

Gabe and I had only ever known how to handle our issues by taking it out on each other. When Dylan acts out, we get frustrated, tired, and angry, and since we can't take it out on him because consequences don't faze him, we take it out on each other. This gets old really fast, but it's hard to break the cycle.

You may be in this exact situation right now: you're in a marriage that is on the rocks, or you're not sure how you and your partner are going to make it through the next year with your child. I don't have all the answers, but I can tell you what helped Gabe and me. We sought counseling, and we did something we'd never done before (and had never crossed our minds until my dear friend Theresa suggested it)—we talked to a pastor.

This was probably the pivotal moment, for me at least. I was able to really release my feelings and admit what I'd been feeling all along: that Dylan's behavior was my fault. It was good for me to hear that this was not possible, that Dylan's make-up and his demeanor were hard-wired into him. It was not my fault that he had turned out this way. For so long I had blamed myself for coming from a broken home and having the genetic makeup of someone who had depression. I felt so much pressure to be the generation that didn't carry on mental illness. Both my mom and dad's sides of their families have rap sheets full of disorders that will just break your heart, and knowing that I was the piece of the puzzle that gave that to my son was just too much for me to bear.

We took a break from marriage counseling, and I eventually started therapy again on my own. I thought talking with a counselor might help me feel a little bit lighter at home, but at first it really only made me feel guilty for leaving Gabe at home with all three kids. BUT, it also opened up an avenue for Dylan to ask me questions about where I was going and why was I going to talk to someone. I decided to tell him the truth, which was that mommy was stressed out and needed to talk to someone to help me be a better mommy.

I really recommend finding a therapist you can talk to, to help you unwind during this stressful time. The best advice I can give you is to try and pinpoint what it is that you need help with. Is it guilt, marriage issues, or family dynamics? It helps to have an idea of where you feel stressed so you can lay out your goals during that first one-on-one with your therapist.

I know finding help for yourself is probably the last thing on your to-do list, but trust me, when you feel better, it will spill over into everything else you do. Take the time to get online, research therapists in your network, and make the call. Make yourself and your well-being a priority, even when you feel like you can't put one foot in front of the other. I know friends and family don't always understand how debilitating it can be to live with a child who is so out of control, but I know that it just takes the fight right out of you sometimes. I know there are days when you just want to give up—I know, because I've had them. Do whatever it is that you need to do to get through another day, whether it's praying, journaling, exercising, or calling a friend.

Sometimes it helps to write down what makes you happy. I know this sounds simple, but it really helps me. Here's an example of one of my many lists:

Elinor's tiny toes	Chapstick
Coffee in the morning	Quiet time
Talking to my gram	Gabe's hugs
Watching a Lifetime movie	Praying
Yoga	

Keep this list where you can see it. I hang mine on my fridge and add to it when I think of something new. Having a tangible piece of paper helps me feel productive about taking care of myself.

13

Moving Past Regrets

"When you're in the thick of raising your kids by yourself, you tend to keep a running list of everything you think you're doing wrong. I recommend taking a lot of family pictures as evidence to the contrary."
– Connie Schultz

One thing you need to know about my son is that he remembers everything. A lot of kids who are autistic, have Asperger's, etc. are very smart. I always think of that scene in the movie *Rain Man* with Dustin Hoffman and Tom Cruise. Hoffman drops the box of toothpicks and starts counting them and amazingly, gets the right number, something only a genius could do. This reminds me of Dylan. I don't think he could necessarily do that, but some of the things he says to me, recalling events from years ago when I never even knew he was listening, amaze and scare me at the same time.

Some memories I'd like to forget. I was never and am still not the corporal punishment type. I spank and did spank my kids for discipline reasons but, as you know, kids with these types of issues do not care. I've always said you could spank Dylan until you were blue in the face, and he wouldn't break down. He'd probably start laughing at you and tell you it didn't hurt. My regrets come from the words I chose to use.

Dylan on his first day of 1st grade

I found that the only thing that would cut Dylan to the core and stop him in his tracks was to tell him exactly what I was thinking. Instead of taking a time-out for myself or stopping to pray, I let the poison in my heart spew from my mouth. Because Dylan has such a good memory, I am often reminded of some of the things I have said to him over the years, and for that I have an enormous amount of guilt, sometimes too much to bear. It's something I have to really pray about, every day. I have to pray that God will change my heart so that words and thoughts like that don't come spilling out.

I go back to James 19-20 (NIV): "My dear brothers and sisters, take note of this: Everyone should be quick to listen, slow to speak and slow to become angry, because human anger does not produce the righteousness that God desires."

This has become my daily mantra. I write it down, I post it wherever I need to, and I remind myself that yes, I am human and I make mistakes...but Dylan will never forget the words I've spoken. Please learn from my mistakes and, if you're like me and you have done things that you are less than proud of, please give yourself grace, change the behavior, and move on. Don't just say you're giving yourself grace. Really, really do it. What does this look like? I can tell you because this is something I've worked really hard to do.

- As hard as it is, think of the things you've said or done that you'd really like to take back and think through those moments. Let them go.

- Read scriptures that help lift you up. A few of my favorites are Matthew, James, and Corinthians. Read these, memorize them, and put them up where you can see them every day.

- Think about what you will say or do before it happens. For example, if I know that Dylan is usually at his worst when I pick him up from school, I will anticipate that and think about how I will react or not react to the things he says and does. Preplanning his discipline and playing out the scene before it happens has really helped me take the focus off verbally hurting him and instead, calmly stating my expectations.

- Tell someone. As embarrassing and as shameful as it feels to have to admit to another person that you regret some of the things you said or did to your child in a moment of rage, there is a feeling of release that comes from it. It was hard, but I told Gabe. I told him some of the things I said to Dylan and that I felt like I was a really bad person. While he agreed with me that the things I said were probably not the best idea, he said he sometimes felt those things too.

- Work really hard at treasuring the small, rare moments that you get with your child when they are in their "element." I love watching Dylan play with Legos and build things that I'd never dreamed of building myself. It's rare to see him sit still and be quiet for any length of time, so when I catch him doing things like this, I stop whatever I'm doing and just observe. I watch, I smile, and sometimes I even snap a picture with my cell phone so I can remind myself that there are good times. My dear friend Theresa reminded me the other day that we must look for God's tiny miracles and blessings throughout the day instead of focusing on what we want Him to do next for us.

14

The Beauty Inside

*"Enjoy the little things. Someday you will
realize they were the big things."*

– Anonymous

I see Dylan. The real him peaks out from time to time and oh, when he does, I savor every moment. When I see him help a little girl who's just fallen on the ground to get up and find the items of her backpack strewn about, I see him. When I overhear him telling his baby sister that he loves her, I see him. When I find him opening the back door to let his dog, Charlie, inside, I know that he cares for his pet. Through all of the bad, there is good. It's like God is shining a light through all of the cracks just so that I can see my son. It's like He's telling me, as lovingly as He can,

"Do you see him? Do you see this beautiful gift I have given you? Go get it. Go get him. And tell him how much he means to you. Don't let his behavior mask who I have made him to be. Go and tell him that he is loved more than he will ever know. Go and hold him, even when he pulls back, because he will remember the mom who tried and not the mom who yelled. Don't be afraid

to look him in the eyes and tell him you're proud of him. Take it. Take every chance and every moment I give you to pour endless amounts of love and wisdom and training into that precious little boy. He was mine before he was yours, and I have given him to you only for a short while. Love him as I have loved you."

That is the frame of mind I try to have most of the time. When I hear myself yelling more than usual or having less patience than normal, I know that I am too far from God's voice, and I need to take time to listen. This has kept me grounded. It is clear to me that I am the exact mom that God made me to be for Dylan, and when I doubt that, question that, or forget that, I go back to the truth: God's Word.

The beauty inside of Dylan is always there. It's these awful diagnoses that have hidden it and made it hard to see. I remember the way Dylan was with his first dog, Bailey. The two of them had an amazing bond, and I would catch Dylan trying to pull himself up to the couch when he was little, just so he could pet her. I remember standing in the kitchen, in our very first home, and watching the two of them sit in front of the back door, just looking outside. It was a boy and his dog, without a care in the world. I'd be getting dinner ready, and Dylan would scoot on over to Bailey. Bailey would sit and wait ever so patiently, knowing that Dylan would make his way over to her and that, when he did, she would get an all-time, best-ever tummy rub. Dylan would look up at me, raspberries bubbling out of his mouth, big blue eyes beaming with happiness, and flash me a rare smile that would melt my heart. It was those moments that I was able to hang onto, so that I could do it all over again another day.

I also remember a rare time with my grandparents. We lived in Missouri at the time, and they live in Massachusetts, so we didn't get to see them very often. Gabe, Dylan, and I drove the twenty-six or so hours it took to get to their house, and then we spent some much needed time with my family. It was summer, right around my birthday (so the middle of June), and Dylan was sitting on the kitchen floor in front of the pellet stove. My grandparents' rocking chairs were on each side of the stove. Everyone was talking, catching up, and nibbling on food, and I looked over at my grandpa who was relaxed in his chair with one hand underneath his chin. He was mesmerized. I watched him, and then followed his gaze down to my son who was taking little toys and hiding them behind his back. Of course, they weren't really hidden because I could see them behind his back, but he would take a toy, move it behind his back, and then reach for another toy. Once all of the toys were behind his back, he would start the process all over again. I followed my grandpa's gaze back up to his eyes and caught a silent laugh and a big smile whenever Dylan did this. It was such a great moment. To know that my family was enjoying my son just as much as I had wanted them to was something I had hoped for. Not having control of your child's behavior can be extremely nerve-wracking and can stop even the most confident parent from doing things. I was just so happy to see that, even though we had our many tough moments, there were good ones too.

Now that Dylan is getting older, it's like he is becoming this little man. I mean, he's not a man yet, obviously, but he is becoming older beyond his years. Sometimes he does things or says things that surprise me. I find myself thinking, wow, is that my son? I had a parent/teacher conference last week and had to hold back my tears when his first grade teacher told me that he had been reading every day to a little girl in his class who was in ESL (English as a Second Language), doing his best to help her learn. What? MY Dylan? I can't even get him to read at home! She assured me, yep, Dylan is reading to her and he's doing great! Now that report was enough to hold me over through spring break!

There are moments—sometimes they don't feel like enough, but they always are—moments that remind me what a beautiful child my son is. Moments that remind me how blessed I am to be his mother. Your child is the same. Every child is the same. There is beauty and wonder and amazement in them all. You must be intentional about seeing what these things are. When you find one, write it down, and put it somewhere where you will see it every day. It will be a great reminder, and a truthful reminder, that there are good things in your child.

I also take pictures. If I catch Dylan doing something that relaxes him (like coloring), or I find him deep in thought while building something out of Legos, I sneak a picture and keep it on my phone to look at, at a later time. Sometimes I even print those pictures out and tuck them in places so I can see them when I need them most…like in the pocket of my purse, the back pocket of my jeans, my keychain, the inside of my car visor. These are all intentional places for me to appreciate Dylan and stare at his handsome little face for as long as I want to.

PART TWO

There's more to you than just being the parent to a child with a disability, even though sometimes it feels like there isn't.

Let's get real: our lives are challenging. Sometimes it's hard to even think about getting out of bed, hard to think about doing the same thing from yesterday all over again, praying deep inside for different results. I know. I've been there. But I've also learned some tricks along the way that I think can help you find your strength and find yourself. I encourage you to try the advice in the following five chapters, because I truly think it will help you go from feeling overwhelmed to in control, no matter what your situation may be.

And remember—you can't help others when you're empty. Don't forget that serving yourself is also a service to others, because it helps you be the best that you can be.

Prayer

"Be the person you needed when you were younger."

– Anonymous

Prayer has been one of the most powerful things for me. When I didn't know if I could make it through another day, I would pray in the shower. Sometimes my son was in his exer-saucer, and other times I was able to have a few minutes alone if I showered at night when my husband was home. Just talking to God about what I was feeling and opening up that dialogue to tell Him what I needed made me feel like I had the strength to parent again the next day. My MOPS group made scripture cards that I was able to put up in random places to help me stay focused. I quickly found which ones were my favorites.

Philippians 4:13 (NKJV) - "I can do all things through Christ who strengthens me." This was one I would recite over and over and over again to get me through the next day, sometimes the next minute. Once I was in Walmart and Dylan was screaming in one of the aisles. I had told him to stop, tried every trick in the book, and he just wasn't listening. I couldn't go on like that, so I knelt down on the floor, closed my eyes, and started saying this verse in my head. When I opened my eyes, Dylan was looking at me very nervously and asked me what I was doing. While I didn't intend for my physical stature in prayer to be the thing that stopped him in his tracks—it was and it did, and I felt much better after it.

Matthew 11:28-30 (NIV) - "Come to me all you who are weary and I will give you rest. For my burden is easy and my yoke is light..." This verse would give me hope when I was dog-tired every night, every morning, and every day, trying to keep up with Dylan's mood swings while also trying to be a good wife and parent to two other children. I would dream about going to a hotel where no one would know me, renting a room, and just holing up under the covers for days—or maybe just one night of uninterrupted sleep. Seriously, I longed to do this for many, many years.

Isaiah 41:10 (NIV) - "I will uphold you with My righteous right hand." This verse spoke to me when I felt conflicted about discipline. Should I spank? Should I do Love & Logic? What's right for my family? I felt pulled in so many directions because I was looking for advice in so many areas. When God called me to this verse, I knew it was meant for me to have confidence in the knowledge that He would show me the way. He would help me be the best parent I could be, if I just came to Him with my hurts.

Philippians 4:6 (NLT) - "Don't worry about anything." Before Dylan came into our family, I never really considered myself someone who worried all that much. But let me just tell you this...when you start getting into weekly doctors' appointments and med checks, you become nervous, and you start to worry about everything. I was sick to my stomach—literally. Sick. To.

My. Stomach. The night that we gave Dylan his very first round of medicine? I barely slept. My mind was racing, and my heart was breaking with the weight and the guilt of giving my child something that was going to alter his behavior and potentially change his personality. I was an absolute wreck. This verse gave me a sense of peace about giving my fears over to God. Not just saying that I would entrust my fears to Him—but really letting go and letting God rule.

James 1:19 (NLT) - "You must all be quick to listen, slow to speak..." This was a verse that really convicted me. It helped me think about the words I was using with Dylan as a reaction to his behavior. I realized I was reacting quickly, not actually waiting and listening, and then correcting. It has also helped me in my marriage. So often I would bark back at Gabe if my feelings had been hurt, or I would be quick to say something that I knew would upset him just to get a reaction. When I'm feeling down or hurt or unloved, I pray this verse, and my heart does the talking instead of my head. It helps put things into perspective, and things become clearer. I have found that it is much, much harder to listen than it is to speak. I work hard to choose my words wisely now, because I know the damage words can do to a sweet little boy's soul, as well as a grown man's heart, and those are two people who I never ever want to hurt again.

These are my favorite verses, but the point is that they've spoken to me in my moment of need. Find verses that speak to you! Write them down, say them out loud, and try to memorize them. The more scripture you can recite, the better equipped you will be when you're facing personal trials. If you don't know where to look, kind of like me when I was just starting to read the Bible, go to a Bible study and ask questions. Look in the back of your Bible where you can look up specific scriptures. Don't overwhelm yourself. Don't think you have to know every piece of scripture to get it right. Just pick one thing and look for it. God will do the rest.

Don't forget to include prayer warriors. Find a close friend that you can pray with or that you can ask to pray for you. It's really important to know that others are lifting you and your family up. Don't be ashamed to ask for prayer. Everyone has struggles, and we weren't meant to fight them alone. We were meant to lift each other up and were designed to live in community with one another. If you don't feel like talking, send a quick email to someone and say, *Hey, I could use some prayer. I'm having a hard time today.*

Have an Accountability Friend

"I'm going out with my 'Get Down Girls'."

– *My grandmother*

When I wrote the last chapter that you should have someone you could shoot a quick email to in your time of need, what person popped to mind? For me, it's my good friend, Theresa. You might remember from earlier in the book that I met her when we lived on the same street in Missouri, and both of our boys were about six months old. They both had acid reflux, and we would talk about our sleepless nights over cups of coffee in her living room. This was my lifeline. We still talk to this day, about parenting and other things going on in our lives. She's invaluable to me. You need a Theresa too. You need at least one person, preferably someone who is going through the same things, to talk with and confide in.

There are times when Theresa has tried to call me for a few days in a row. I see her calls, but I don't or can't answer. She will usually text me, email me, or heck, probably smoke-screen me a message just to reach me and ask if I'm okay. Why? Because Theresa knows I have depression. She knows that sometimes I don't feel like talking. But you know what else she knows? That I need her. That even though sometimes I just want to be left alone, sometimes it's just as important that I'm not left alone. She is my accountability friend. If you don't have one, you need one. Having trouble deciding who that should be? Make a list if you need to. Write down your friends' names and your family members' names, and pray over that list. Who is God asking you to seek out? It could even be someone at your church, maybe an older woman who is more mature in her faith. It's okay to be vulnerable, and it's okay to ask for prayer.

My dear friend Theresa. The one I chased down with my stroller.

I've seen therapists for most of my life, the details of which could fill a whole 'nother book. But the difference between past therapists I've had and the ones that I look for now is very simple: their faith. It's important to me that if I do see a counselor, it's someone I can talk to about where God fits in my life. I need them to know that walking in faith is just as important as navigating the medical system.

Another tip? Find a support group. I used to think that there would be a support group around every corner if I needed one. But there wasn't. There wasn't even one. This may have had something to do with the size of the town I lived in, but nonetheless, a support group or some type of support system is a must. Find one or maybe even create one.

I'm a go-getter, so at one time I thought about starting a support group for moms with children who had behavioral challenges similar to my son's. Then I thought, *Heck, I can barely get through one day! Right now is not the time for me to start a group!* Instead, I found other ways to get the support I needed. I wrote things down in my journal so that I could look back one day and see how far we'd all come. I searched for online support groups where I could be more anonymous, because let's face it, none of us really want to admit that our child is different. I found groups mostly on Facebook like Sensory Processing Disorder Parent Support, Amy Vaughan's Positively Sensory, The Sensory Spectrum, Support for Parents of Children with ADD/ADHD, Oppositional Defiant Disorder Parent, Parenting Kids with Anxiety, and Rantings of an ADHD Mom. Type in the key word of what you're looking for and you're bound to find something that sparks your interest.

When Gabe and I were going through a really rough time in our marriage, we reached out to a pastoral friend who agreed to sit down with us and counsel us. Things came out in that meeting that neither one of us had ever heard from the other. To be blunt, it was an eye-opener for me. There were several things that the pastor said to us that still roll around in my head, and I often use them to help us get back on track and stay focused on nurturing our marriage. No matter what your trial is, or what your family dynamics are, it is so important to get help and communicate with someone. When we stuff everything inside and try to do life alone, bad feelings start to manifest. Before we know it, our whole world is falling apart, and we ask ourselves, "How did I get here?"

Don't wait until you feel like everything is falling apart! Find an accountability partner and call them. Set up a time and a place to talk. It's the first best step you can take in nurturing yourself. And who doesn't want to be the best version of ourselves?

Grab Some Alone Time

"I dream my painting and then I paint my dream."
– Van Gogh

I'm an extrovert by nature, just like my dad. I always tell people that my dad has never met a stranger, so I know just where my social skills come from. I am proud of that because it's something that makes me unique, but at the same time, I crave alone time too.

Remember when I said you can't fill others when you're empty? I know that it sometimes goes against a mother's nature to put herself first, but at times you have to. If you're burned out, what can you offer your family? One way to combat the burnout is to grab some time alone. I know this is hard, but I wish I had made it a priority when I was in my earlier years of parenting. At the time, I just didn't know how I could manage "me time" without having any family around. I know better now, though, and want to encourage you to do what I didn't: look into Mother's Day Out programs or MOPS chapters. Joining my local MOPS groups was

Blowing out candles for my 33rd birthday. I remember thinking to myself, "This will be the year I get back to me..."

the first time I was able to carve out time for myself. It helped me feel human again. The best way to find these groups is to ask around (specifically, other moms) or type in "Mother's Day Out Programs" in your search engine.

For me, I came up with what I call "Meagan Days," where I make the day all about me and fill it with things that I love. For example, I love the spa. So, a typical Meagan Day might be booking an appointment for a facial (my absolute favorite service to get). I love learning about my skin and how to take better care of it. I like having a professional spend an hour on my face, getting it clean and super sparkly. It makes me feel special, and it makes me feel like I'm actually doing something good for my body. I also love stationary stores. They're kind of hard to find nowadays since everything is online, but I'm never in a happier place than when I track one down. There's something about being in a place completely dedicated to all things paper, accessories, and frills. I love it! Actually, a teeny tiny dream of mine has always been to open up my own store where I bring in beautiful paper from all over the world. (Bucket list. We'll get to that later.)

Basically, when we fill ourselves up with good things and things that fulfill our wants and needs and down-right basic necessities of life, we can then turn around and be that healthy person for someone else, like a family member, a close friend, your spouse, or maybe the person who gets on your nerves from time to time. When we feel complete and whole and at peace, that confidence and self-nurturing can then be seen by others. Taking care of yourself isn't just good for you. It's necessary so that you can be the best mom, wife, daughter, sister, and friend that you desire to be.

I can always tell when I need a break: when I start to snap at my kids over trivial things; when I'm short with Gabe; when I don't take the time to return people's phone calls; when I'm tired; when my body and bones are achy; when I feel like I'm coming down with a cold; when my to-do list is out of control; when I don't have a moment in my day to allow spontaneous things to happen; when I can't see the three little blessings standing right in front of me; when my eyes start to wander from my husband to other things; when my head starts making decisions instead of my heart; when I stop doing kind things for others; when I'm talking about my problems more than I'm praying about them. THESE. These are my red flags and I know I must do a 180 to turn things around.

There were many times in my early years as a parent when I needed a break. I remember feeling like I was never going to stop breastfeeding. It was wonderful that I was able to do it, but it definitely tied me to my child at all times—especially Dylan, since he had GERD. I used to pray that God would let him sleep for just an hour. Just one hour at a time so that I could get one extra hour of sleep. I used to dream about what it would be like to lock my bedroom door, hide under the covers, pull the shades, close the curtains, and have the house be completely silent. One can dream, right? If that's where you are right now, please, know that I am shouting as loudly as I can to you...

YOU NEED A BREAK!

You will be better for it. If you don't know how to get a break, start with one hour. Tell your spouse that you need just one hour of alone time. Get in the car and lay down, if that's the only quiet place you can find. Whatever you need to do to get some peace and quiet, go do it. You'll be better for it.

Make a To-Do List

> *"The decisions you make determine the schedule you keep. The schedule you keep determines the life you live. And how you live your life determines how you spend your soul."*
>
> – *Lysa Terkeurst*, The Best Yes

This is one of my favorites. I am big on to-do lists because, if we break things down into bite-size pieces, we can accomplish what we need to do without getting overwhelmed. It's when we try to do too much that we lose control. We get short with our kids, we forget to call people back, we snack on food instead of sitting down to eat, and we start to feel bad about ourselves when we should be investing in ourselves. Instead, just keep it simple.

Get yourself a nice planner or a cute notepad (this always gets me excited about tackling my things). Write out everything you think you need to do that day, and then go back over it. Are there a few things you can cross off? Make it manageable. So many times we try to do it all, and we try to be everything for everyone. Take this responsibility off of your list and be realistic. If you have a new baby, your list might look like this:

1. Wake up and eat breakfast
2. Play and read to baby
3. Shower
4. Cook Dinner

If you have toddlers and preschoolers, your list might look like this:

1. Going to the park
2. Heading to the gym if your gym has child care
3. Picking up the house
4. Running to the post office

What does your to-do list look like? Write it down here:

1. _____

2. _____

3. _____

4. _____

Make a Bucket List

"Conquer your fears. Otherwise, your fears will conquer you."

– Fortune Cookie

I hinted at this one earlier, and it is, by far, my most favorite tip! Make a bucket list. If you don't have one, make one; if you have one, look at it, update it, cross off things you've already done, and add new ones as you think of them. This is a tangible way to see your dreams come true. It's a snapshot of where you were to where you are now. Your bucket list says a lot about you. Here's a peek at mine.

~~Go to Hawaii~~

Run a marathon

Learn to speak French again
(I used to speak this fluently)

~~Have a baby~~

Go skydiving

Visit Yoann's grave
(a friend of mine who passed away)

~~Write a book~~

Write a children's book

~~Go parasailing~~

Go to a shooting range and
learn how to shoot a gun

Visit Jerusalem

Take guitar lessons

Stay married forever

Own a stationary store

My Bucket List

I like to update my list whenever I think of something new or when I have completed something and can check it off. I think this is a fun way to keep my dreams a reality. I think life is way too short not to have goals, because goals keep us on our toes and always reaching for that next thing.

What does your bucket list look like? Don't know where to begin? Think about things you've always wanted to do. Now write them down. You know those things that you've only dreamt about? Yeah, write those down too. How about the things that you used to want to do when you were little? Disneyland? Why not? Who cares if you're an adult now! Want to take voice lessons even though you know you can't sing? This is your life. Take it by the wheel.

Take your bucket list one step further, and join forces with your spouse. What's on his bucket list? What things do you guys want to accomplish together? I guarantee that you will learn something new about your partner that will surprise you. Maybe you have dreams for him and he has dreams for you? Share those with each other and start making them happen.

I asked Gabe recently what was on his bucket list, and he said going cross country on his motorcycle and going to the Masters (golf) with his dad. Two things that I had no clue he ever wanted to do. I've been with this man for fifteen years, and I did not know the only two things he had left to do in his life that were important to him. But now that I do know, we can work together to make those things happen.

The
Overwhelmed-to-In-Control
10-Day Challenge

"Go confidently in the direction of your dreams. Live the life you've imagined."

– Henry David Thoreau

"Overwhelmed schedule, underwhelmed soul."

– Lysa Terkeurst, The Best Yes

Being a mom is hard. So hard that sometimes it's difficult to think about getting up and doing it all over again. "Overwhelmed to In Control" is a ten-day series that I have put together to help you get up and out of bed day after day. The following ten tips will encourage you to get the strength you need to flourish as a mom.

For those of you who have children with special needs, this challenge will be especially helpful for you. I know. Been there, still doing that! I know your time is valuable, so I promise to keep each challenge short and simple. I also promise that each challenge will be packed with helpful information that you can use long after the challenge is over.

DAY 1 – Marbles in My Head

Welcome to the first day of your 10-day challenge. Marbles—those little glass balls our kids play with and we can't stand to pick up, right? Well, in this exercise, I'm not talking about real marbles like the ones mentioned above. I'm talking about all of those little nuggets of thoughts, ideas, worries, and hang-ups that are floating and bouncing around inside your head. The ones that sometimes come out as mumble-jumble to anyone who might be in our listening path. I'm talking about the marble that says you felt sad today when your son said he had no friends. The marble that says you aren't in the mood for sex…again. The marble that says you really need to call that friend of yours who called you like three months ago. Take all of those marbles and write them down or verbally tell them to your spouse. This is a great opportunity for you to take a walk or sit down on the couch together. Literally say to your spouse, "Honey, I have some marbles in my head and I need to get them out." You will feel so much better when those marbles are out of your head! Remember, a weight is always easier when two people help to carry it.

DAY 2 – Make a List

List out every single thing you can think of that's bothering you or every single thing you want to do this year. Those children's books you wanted to write? Write that down. Those hair bows you wanted to start making and sell? Write that down too. The point of today's exercise is to take those big dreams and break them down into bite-sized pieces. Often, when we have such big ideas, we can feel bogged down, almost like a failure, because we never get any traction on the things we really want to do. We can start to look at ourselves in the mirror and wonder how we went from big-city girl to small-town mom. It's easy to get overwhelmed, so write down your thoughts and ideas on the worksheet provided in the back of the book, no matter how big or small. It might be getting your daughter signed up for preschool or scheduling your next haircut. But whatever it is, only fill out the first column in the worksheet. The following columns will be for tomorrow's challenge.

DAY 3 – Prioritize Your Thoughts and Ideas

Go back to yesterday's worksheet and put a 1, 2, or 3 next to each idea. The number one would mean that it's something urgent that needs to be done right away. The number two would be something that you'd like to do soon (maybe in a week's time) but that does not have to be done immediately. A number three would be something you would like to do in the near future. This might be something like running a 5k. Once you have each idea numbered, go ahead and fill out the next three columns with each step needed to move yourself in the right direction. This is going to take some thinking, so be patient with yourself and keep it simple. This exercise isn't meant to overwhelm you, but rather to break big things into smaller, more doable actions. Finally, the last column: decide on a date. Today, tomorrow, next week, next month, etc. But give yourself a deadline! This will help you turn those ideas into accomplishments.

DAY 4 – Pick One Thing to Accomplish Today

Grab your list and pick one thing you would like to accomplish today. If you've just had a baby, your list is going to look a lot different than someone whose children are just starting school. That's okay. Maybe your goal for today is to take a shower. Not just a one-minute shower, but a long, hot, lovely shower where you get to shave your legs and you know, wash your hair for the first time this week. For you more seasoned moms, maybe your one thing today will be to call a friend to meet for coffee. Go ahead. Pick one thing and do it. Make sure you check it off your list so that you can see your personal accomplishments!

DAY 5 – Marbles Need to Be Shared

Remember those pesky marbles? Yeah, you're not off the hook just yet. I heard a pastor say that the average American couple spends twenty-seven minutes a week talking to their spouse. Twenty-seven minutes! Is it any wonder that sometimes we can feel alone in our struggles? Just in case you didn't get the chance to share those marbles with your spouse yet, I've got ten ways you can fit that in right now. Share your marbles when you:

- Take a walk after work
- Eat dinner together
- Snuggle before bed
- Are out on a date night
- Text (yes, I do this to my husband)
- Email (yep, this too!)
- Call each other in the middle of the day
- Write notes or letters to one another
- Cook dinner together, or work together to complete a chore or between commercials when you're both on the couch watching TV

DAY 6 – Go to Bed Early Tonight

Most of the time, we're just tired. Plain old tired. Kids are exhausting and getting them and ourselves into bed can feel like such a daunting task. Once you've established a bedtime routine that works for your family, make it a priority to put yourself to bed too. Resist the urge to do just one more thing and instead, lie down and close your eyes. Feeling overwhelmed leads to stress, which leads to physical symptoms, which leads to so many other things. Do yourself a favor and go to bed early. Give your body the rest it needs.

Overwhelmed:
TO AFFECT (SOMEONE) VERY STRONGLY, TO CAUSE (SOMEONE) TO HAVE TOO MANY THINGS TO DEAL WITH, TO DEFEAT (SOMEONE OR SOMETHING) COMPLETELY*

DAY 7 – Clear One Day off Your Calendar

Take a look at your calendar. If you have something written in every square, try to eliminate one of those squares. Is it really necessary to get the dog groomed this week? Can it wait until next week when you only have one or two things going on? Be realistic. If a packed schedule overwhelms you, take back control and rearrange a few things on your calendar to even your days out. You'll be amazed at how odd (but nice) it feels when you have a completely blank space on your calendar. It leaves room for fun!

*Source: Merriam-Webster's Learner's Dictionary

DAY 8 – Turn Off Your Phone

Okay, okay, this might not be possible if you have kids in school, but you can at least put it in another room while you do other things. I always think, what would my grandma have done if she'd had a phone with her at all times? There was no such thing as a cell phone in her day, and yet she was able to go about her day just as well as you and I do these days. Leaving your phone in a neutral area where you're not prone to hear every ding, ring, or buzz can really have a calming and peaceful effect. This is one of the best ways to go from overwhelmed to in control.

DAY 9 – Move Your Body

Some of us hate to work out. I get it. I have to be in the mood to go for a run or take a gym class, but I am telling you, incorporating movement into your day is so beneficial to your health. If you suffer from postpartum depression or have had depression in the past, you know how hard it can be to just get out of bed, let alone go to the gym. It's proven that we need certain levels of vitamin D in our bodies. Vitamin D releases a hormone called *oxytocin* (the happy factor). The higher the levels of oxytocin, the happier you will be. Call a friend and see if she can meet up with you for a walk. Grab the stroller and take a ten-minute walk around the neighborhood. One of my best friends today is someone I met while on a walk around my subdivision. (Love you, T!)

DAY 10 – Try a New Recipe

This is a good one. We all have a million cookbooks, random magazine rip-outs, or Pinterest pins of things that look yummy. Pick one and make it today. If you're trying to bounce back after having a baby or are trying to get in shape, you will surely benefit from a simple eating plan to help you stay on track. Let's be real: it's inevitable that we're going to finish our kid's grilled cheese or take a swipe of their candy when they're not looking. Thinking about eating healthy is definitely overwhelming, so where does one begin? Oftentimes, we think we have to cut out something entirely just to be healthy, but I have always said that anything in moderation is just fine. Take a look at this sample of a healthy eating plan that almost any person can work from. Adjust it to fit your needs or use it as is.

The Basics for Heathly Eating, Paleo-ish

 Eat:
Meat, fish, eggs, vegetables, fruits, nuts, seeds, herbs, spices, healthy fats and oils

 Avoid:
Processed foods, sugar, soft drinks, most grains, most dairy products, legumes, artificial sweeteners, vegetable oils, margarine, and trans-fats

 What do drink:
Water, tea, or black coffee

One trick I use to spend more time with my family and less time in the kitchen is to cook a big enough dinner in order to use the leftovers for lunch the following day.

Another is to prepare some of the foods that I am going to eat on Sunday, like chopping up vegetables or grilling the chicken in advance.

A healthy breakfast could like this:
Scrambled eggs with a side of blueberries, add in some oatmeal if you are not eliminating all grains from your diet

Bacon and eggs

Lunch could be:
Chicken salad made with olive oil mayo over baby spinach. Add a handful of almonds

Leftovers from the night before

Dinner could look like:
Steak (or fish), baked asparagus, and cauliflower rice

Ground beef stir fry with vegetables

Paleo Snacks:
Hard boiled eggs

Nuts

A piece of fruit

Carrots

Leftovers from dinner

(Meal plan provided by Donald Longley, RD)

Now that you've been through these ten challenges, I hope you're feeling more in control of your life. You'll notice that these techniques are adaptable to you, and you might have even come up with some of your own. The important thing is that you TAKE CHARGE of something each day. Often we feel overwhelmed, so do something you know you can control, and it will give the entire day a better feel.

Below is a sample of how to use the Overwhelmed to In Control Worksheets.
Photocopy the following pages for your personal use or
visit www.meaganruffing.com to download a printable version.

OVERWHEMING THOUGHT/FEELING: *Should I put Hannah in preschool?* 1

URGENCY: *1* *1 = Now, 2 = Sometime Soon, 3 = In the Future*

FIRST STEP: *Research schools, ask around*

SECOND STEP: *Set up tours at 1 - 2 schools. Decide which school I want her to go to.*

THIRD STEP: *Register*

SUGGESTED COMPLETION DATE: *As soon as possible!*

OVERWHEMING THOUGHT/FEELING: _____ **1**

URGENCY: _____ *1 = Now, 2 = Sometime Soon, 3 = In the Future*

FIRST STEP: _____

SECOND STEP: _____

THIRD STEP: _____

SUGGESTED COMPLETION DATE: _____

OVERWHEMING THOUGHT/FEELING: _____ **2**

URGENCY: _____ *1 = Now, 2 = Sometime Soon, 3 = In the Future*

FIRST STEP: _____

SECOND STEP: _____

THIRD STEP: _____

SUGGESTED COMPLETION DATE: _____

OVERWHEMING THOUGHT/FEELING: _____ **3**

URGENCY: _____ *1 = Now, 2 = Sometime Soon, 3 = In the Future*

FIRST STEP: _____

SECOND STEP: _____

THIRD STEP: _____

SUGGESTED COMPLETION DATE: _____

OVERWHEMING THOUGHT/FEELING: _____ **4**

URGENCY: _____ *1 = Now, 2 = Sometime Soon, 3 = In the Future*

FIRST STEP: _____

SECOND STEP: _____

THIRD STEP: _____

SUGGESTED COMPLETION DATE: _____

AS FOR ME AND MY HOUSE, WE WILL SERVE THE LORD.

Joshua 24:15 (NASB)

BE KIND TO ONE ANOTHER AND BUILD EACH OTHER UP.

I Thessalonians 5:11

Photocopy the following pages and cut out each card for your personal use.

CREATE IN ME A PURE HEART, AND RENEW A STEADFAST SPIRIT WITHIN ME.

Psalm 51:10 (KJV)

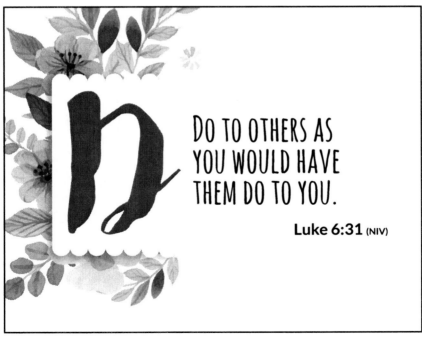

DO TO OTHERS AS YOU WOULD HAVE THEM DO TO YOU.

Luke 6:31 (NIV)

E

EVERY KNEE WILL BOW
BEFORE ME; EVERY TONGUE
WILL ACKNOWLWDGE ME.

Romans 14:11 (NIV)

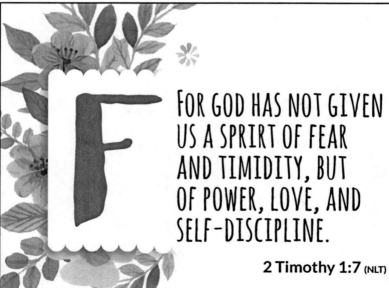

F

FOR GOD HAS NOT GIVEN
US A SPRIRT OF FEAR
AND TIMIDITY, BUT
OF POWER, LOVE, AND
SELF-DISCIPLINE.

2 Timothy 1:7 (NLT)

Photocopy the following pages and cut out each card for your personal use.

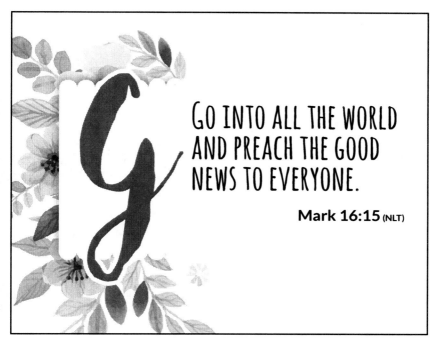

GO INTO ALL THE WORLD AND PREACH THE GOOD NEWS TO EVERYONE.

Mark 16:15 (NLT)

HEAR O ISREAL: THE LORD OUR GOD, THE LORD IS ONE.

Deuteronomy 6:4 (NIV)

Visit www.meaganruffing.com to download printable scripture cards.

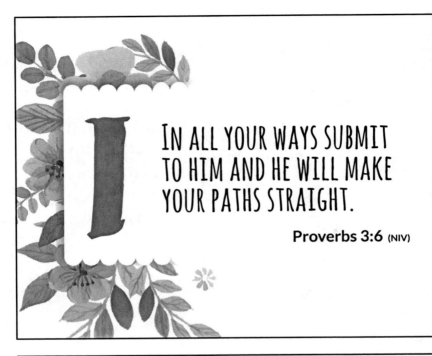

IN ALL YOUR WAYS SUBMIT TO HIM AND HE WILL MAKE YOUR PATHS STRAIGHT.

Proverbs 3:6 (NIV)

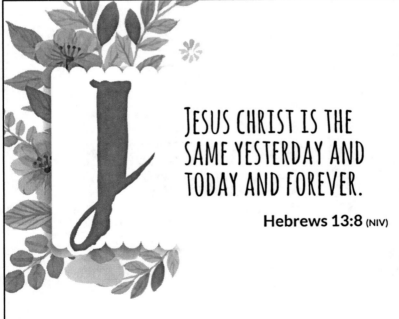

JESUS CHRIST IS THE SAME YESTERDAY AND TODAY AND FOREVER.

Hebrews 13:8 (NIV)

Photocopy the following pages and cut out each card for your personal use.

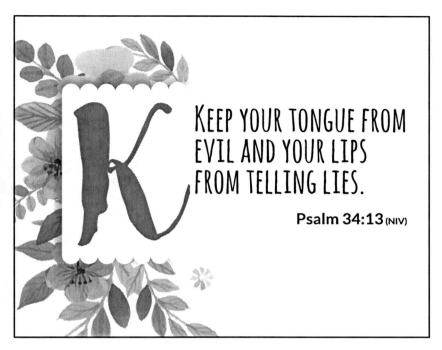

KEEP YOUR TONGUE FROM
EVIL AND YOUR LIPS
FROM TELLING LIES.

Psalm 34:13 (NIV)

LET US LOVE ONE
ANOTHER FOR LOVE
COMES FROM GOD.

I John 4:7 (NIV)

Visit www.meaganruffing.com to download printable scripture cards.

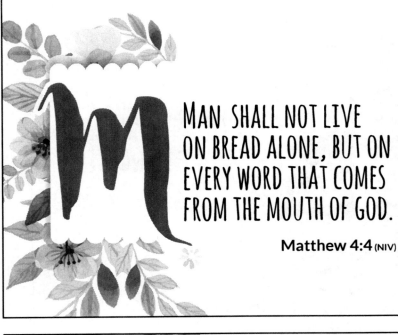

MAN SHALL NOT LIVE ON BREAD ALONE, BUT ON EVERY WORD THAT COMES FROM THE MOUTH OF GOD.

Matthew 4:4 (NIV)

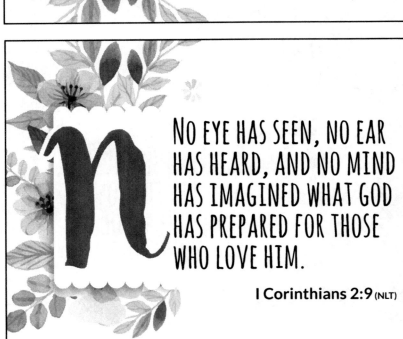

NO EYE HAS SEEN, NO EAR HAS HEARD, AND NO MIND HAS IMAGINED WHAT GOD HAS PREPARED FOR THOSE WHO LOVE HIM.

I Corinthians 2:9 (NLT)

Photocopy the following pages and cut out each card for your personal use.

O God you are my god.
I earnestly search for
you. My soul thirsts
for you.

Psalm 63:1 (NLT)

Praise the lord. Give
thanks to the lord for
he is good; his love
endures forever.

I John 4:7 (NIV)

EVERYONE SHOULD BE QUICK TO LISTEN, SLOW TO SPEAK, AND SLOW TO BECOME ANGRY.

James 1:19 (NIV)

REJOICE IN THE LORD ALWAYS. I WILL SAY IT AGAIN: REJOICE!

Philippians 4:4 (NIV)

Photocopy the following pages and cut out each card for your personal use.

Seek first his kingdom and his rightousness, and all these things will be given to you as well.

Matthew 6:33 (NIV)

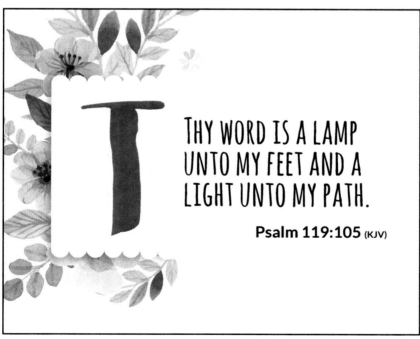

Thy word is a lamp unto my feet and a light unto my path.

Psalm 119:105 (KJV)

Understanding is a fountain of life to one who has it.

Proverbs 16:22 (NASB)

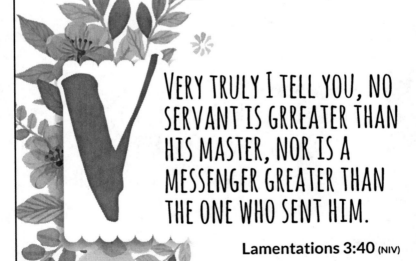

Very truly I tell you, no servant is grreater than his master, nor is a messenger greater than the one who sent him.

Lamentations 3:40 (NIV)

Photocopy the following pages and cut out each card for your personal use.

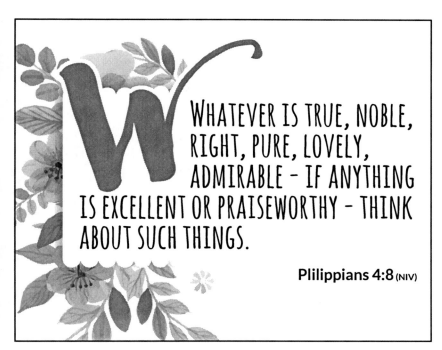

WHATEVER IS TRUE, NOBLE, RIGHT, PURE, LOVELY, ADMIRABLE – IF ANYTHING IS EXCELLENT OR PRAISEWORTHY – THINK ABOUT SUCH THINGS.

Plilippians 4:8 (NIV)

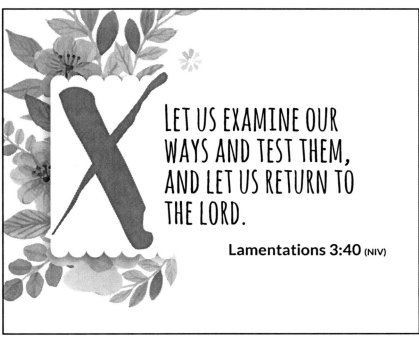

LET US EXAMINE OUR WAYS AND TEST THEM, AND LET US RETURN TO THE LORD.

Lamentations 3:40 (NIV)

You are the light of the world — like a city on a hilltop that cannot be hidden.

Matthew 5:14 (NLT)

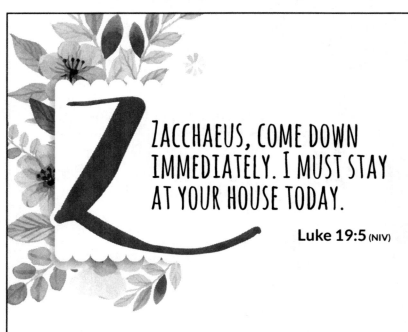

Zacchaeus, come down immediately. I must stay at your house today.

Luke 19:5 (NIV)

Photocopy the following pages and cut out each card for your personal use.

So love the lord your god with all your heart, soul, and strength. Memorize his laws and tell them to your children over and over again. Talk about them all the time, whether you're at home or walking along the road or going to bed at night, or getting up in the morning.

Deuteronomy 6:5-7 (CEV)

REFERENCES:

1, 2, 3 Magic
www.123magic.com
Recommended reading: 1-2-3 Magic: Effective Discipline for Children 2-12
by Thomas W. Phelan, Ph.D

Itsy Bitsy Yoga
www.yokid.org
Recommended reading: Itsy Bitsy Yoga: Poses to Help Your Baby Sleep
Longer, Digest Better, and Grow Stronger by Helen Garabedian

Love & Logic
www.loveandlogic.com
Recommended reading: Parenting with Love & Logic
by Foster Cline, MD and Jim Fay

Mothers of Preschoolers (MOPS)
www.mops.org

Positively Sensory
Positively Sensory!: A Guide to Help Your Child Develop Positive Approaches
to Learning and Cope with Sensory Processing Difficulty
by Amy Vaughan

Writer Mama by Christina Katz
www.christinakatz.com

CPSIA information can be obtained
at www.ICGtesting.com
Printed in the USA
FFOW05n0230041116